D0017661

One-Minute
PRAYERS®
for HUSBANDS

NICK HARRISON

HARVEST HOUSE PUBLISHERS
EUGENE, OREGON

ONE-MINUTE PRAYERS® FOR HUSBANDS
Copyright © 2017 by Nick Harrison
Published by Harvest House Publishers
Eugene, Oregon 97402
www.harvesthousepublishers.com

ISBN 978-0-7369-7272-7 (pbk.)
ISBN 978-0-7369-7273-4 (eBook)

Printed in China

18 19 20 21 22 23 24 25 / RDS-GL / 10 9 8 7 6 5

To husbands everywhere

INTRODUCTION

Men, God has given us a tremendous calling as husbands. He's also made it a bit easier by giving us wives we love and with whom we want to spend the rest of our lives. Still, there are challenges, aren't there? Leading without dominating, listening without commenting, denying ourselves, all these and so much more.

But when God calls, he enables. He has given us the abilities and the strength to carry out our husbandly assignment. My hope is that the following pages will help us become better husbands and more Christ-like men.

Each page includes a Scripture verse, an observation about the topic, and a suggested prayer. Keep in mind that though each page will take about a minute to read and pray, no one's watching the clock. I hope these short prayers will serve as a jump-start for you to pray on, tailoring your petitions to your specific needs.

Finally, as I was mentioning to my wife over lunch, there are some topics that are repeated. When I told her what those topics were—communication, leadership, pride, protection, and a few others—she insisted that the repetition was a good thing and I should keep those topics repeated in the book. As a good husband, I listened to my wife.

May God be with you as you read and pray—and may God bless your marriage!

The Golden Rule of Marriage

*As you wish that others would
do to you, do so to them.*
LUKE 6:31

Marriage is a lifelong course in selflessness. Many of us get a low grade on the first few pop quizzes we face. But we can be quick learners when we want to be. Such is the case by simply living with our spouse according to the Golden Rule of "as you wish that others would do to you, do so to them" as our mission statement.

Practice makes perfect. Another pop quiz is just on the horizon. Be prepared.

Father, help me to do for my wife those things I would want her to do for me. Help me anticipate her needs before they're apparent. Enable me as I continue this course in unselfishness called Marriage 101. I pray you'll bless our marriage with mutual selflessness, deepening our love for one another—and for you.

You, as Leader

Husbands, live with your wives in an understanding way, showing honor to the woman as the weaker vessel, since they are heirs with you of the grace of life, so that your prayers may not be hindered.
1 Peter 3:7

Leadership doesn't come easily to many husbands. At least not the kind of leadership that includes tact, humility, and preferring our wives over ourselves. And yet true family leadership for a husband is all about just that—selflessness. The great thing is that most wives respond overwhelmingly to leadership that serves. They also balk at a prideful leader who won't communicate effectively or who refuses to listen to their wisdom.

God, help me to be the leader our family needs. Give me wisdom beyond my normal abilities. Guide me in decision-making that affects our family. Remind me to listen to my wife when she shares her insight with me. Teach me how to lead through serving and to serve through leading. As I guide our family, I pray you will lead me to follow closely the path you've blazed for us.

THE HUSBAND AS HELPER

*The LORD God said, "It is not good
that the man should be alone;
I will make him a helper fit for him."*
GENESIS 2:18

When Eve was created, it's noted she was a "helper" to Adam. But does that mean Adam wasn't also a helper to Eve? Yes, he was. Husbands serve their wives by helping them in any way they can. They're there for them. Where does your wife need your help now? If you don't know, ask her.

God, it is truly not good for man to live alone, so thank you for providing me with a helper. As such, I know that I'm also to help her in her role as wife and mother. I pray I would become more observant to her needs and to ways I can be there for her. Even today show me how I can be of help to my wife.

Bring us closer together, Lord. Help us to always remember that each of us is a helper fit for each other.

Time Alone Together

My beloved is mine, and I am his.
Song of Solomon 2:16

We live in an age when both husbands and wives are busy. Often, both partners work outside the home. After work there can be distractions: housework (for both him and her), kids, bills to pay, errands to run...and more. Busyness can be an enemy of even a good marriage. It can destroy intimacy and hinder true communication. Good husbands make sure there's daily time to be alone with their wives. Schedule it if necessary, but consider it vital to your marriage. If you are too busy for time alone with your wife, you're too busy—period.

Lord, amid all the distractions my wife and I face, I pray you'll keep us mindful of our need to get alone often and share our lives with each other. Time alone to be in each other's presence, time to enjoy the gifts each of us brings to the other. And in these times alone, I pray we would remember and welcome your presence as part of our love.

Your Wife's Encourager

Encourage one another and build one another up.
1 Thessalonians 5:11

Husbands love it when their wives encourage them. Face it, we all love it when the most important person in our life comes alongside and tells us we can do it—whatever "it" is. But who will encourage our wives, if not us? When a woman marries a man, she wants him to be many things to her…and one of those things is to be an encourager. She needs to be told she can do "it" too.

Lord, help me be aware of those moments when my wife needs my encouragement. Help me say the words that will get her over the hump when she's at a standstill. Give me compassion for her during her hard times and wisdom to know when to just love her and not say anything. Help me build her up in the faith too, Lord. Help me encourage her to rely on you to fulfill your destiny for her. Lord, bless my wife.

A SHARED LIFE

"The two shall become one flesh." So they
are no longer two but one flesh.
MARK 10:8

In a Christian marriage, two become one. That's God's divine arithmetic: one plus one equals one. Many marriages fail because one or both partners bring their worst "self" into the marriage instead of laying down what was their single life in favor of a newly shared life. Sharing is essential in marriage...and the most important thing you can bring to share in your marriage is your very life.

Father, thank you that you've called my wife and me into oneness. You have taken the two of us as separate individuals and fashioned us as one. Help us both to see each other as part of the one new flesh we've become. Lord, be the center of our "one flesh" being. Let nothing come between us, dividing us into two again. Breathe your life into us, and fill us with your Spirit.

LOOKING AHEAD

I know the plans I have for you, declares the LORD,
plans for welfare and not for evil, to
give you a future and a hope.
JEREMIAH 29:11

Where you are now in your marriage is not where you want to be five years from now...or even one year from now. You want your marriage to grow, blossom, mature. God can bring about the necessary circumstances that will cause your marriage to deepen. Talk to your wife about how she and you both want to be in the future. Look ahead with optimism for your marriage. Then take the small daily steps that will take you both where you want to be.

Heavenly Father, you have a plan for our marriage—a *perfect* plan. Your desire is to move us along the pathway of your will with contentment, accomplishment, and mutual joy. I pray you'll guide us as we make our way through what seems to natural eyes as an uncertain future. In reality, it's a promising future that will take us both to the place you want us to be. By faith, Lord, we look ahead with confidence.

A Solitary Eye

He who commits adultery lacks sense;
he who does it destroys himself.
PROVERBS 6:32

When we were single we walked through life with both eyes scouring the landscape for our desired future partner. Who would we marry? Would it work out? Will she be pretty? And then, in time, we met the right woman. At that point, our vision necessarily narrowed considerably. Now we see through a solitary eye. We love only her. We will always love only her. There is no more scouring of the landscape. God has gifted us with the right woman to spend our life with. Love her—and *only* her.

Dear God, in our highly sexed culture, virtually any man can be tempted to cheat on his wife. Lord, strengthen me if and when such temptation comes to me. Remind me that this wonderful woman is your choice for me—your *only* choice for me until death do us part. Keep me far from the destructive force called adultery. Help me in my resolve to stay faithful not only with my actions, but also with my eyes.

Taking Your Wife's Side

*Two are better than one, because they
have a good reward for their toil.*
Ecclesiastes 4:9

If we enjoy team sports, we understand the importance of working together as a team. Marriage is a lot like that. You and your wife are a team of two. You are on the same side in this game of life. You need to depend on her to be in your corner and you need to stay by her side when trouble comes—and it will. Loyalty to the family team God is building will bring great rewards. You will win the game.

Thank you, Lord, for giving me the teammate for life whom I call my wife. You promise a good reward for our common toil as we go through everything together. I praise you for creating men and women both in need of one another. I thank you that for my need, you chose the woman I now love. I will always remain on her side—just as you remain forever on our side. Yes, Lord, two *are* better than one.

WHAT'S HER LOVE LANGUAGE?

Behold, you are beautiful, my beloved, truly delightful.
SONG OF SOLOMON 1:16

Dr. Gary Chapman was a successful marriage counselor for thirty years before he wrote his now-classic bestseller *The Five Love Languages: The Secret to Love That Lasts*. Dr. Chapman lists the following as love languages that can save marriages:

- Words of Affirmation
- Quality Time
- Receiving Gifts
- Acts of Service
- Physical Touch

Do you know which of these rank high with your wife? Do you know which she counts as less important? The subtitle of Dr. Chapman's book identifies these as a "secret." But now the secret is out. Enriching your love life through your wife's love languages can change your marriage.

Dear Lord, help me learn my wife's love languages. I pray I may be sensitive enough to employ each of these love languages when appropriate. I pray for the wisdom to affirm her verbally, spend quality time with her, offer her gifts, do acts of service, and touch her appropriately. May she respond to each by knowing my love for her.

MONEY MATTERS

Keep your life free from love of money, and
be content with what you have,
for he has said, "I will never
leave you nor forsake you."

HEBREWS 13:5

Many marriages break up over the issue of money—mostly the seeming lack of it. A healthy marriage can result from healthy money management. That may mean putting off desired purchases for a while—maybe a long while. Manage your money wisely and eliminate marital stress over financial difficulties. Resolve to never fight over money. Cultivate the trust of God for your needs.

Lord, I pray you'll help both me and my wife take our eyes off money or material gain as a measurement of success. I pray we'll always look to you to meet our financial needs and that you'll caution us during times when we're tempted to do something monetarily that may put our marriage at risk. Remind us, Father, that our true riches are in you and that we're not to lay up treasures here on earth, but invest instead in spiritual riches in heaven. Lord, be our Provider in all things.

You Married Her Family

*If possible, so far as it depends on
you, live peaceably with all.*
Romans 12:18

When a man marries, he marries not just a wife, but also into an existing family. But loving a woman doesn't always translate into the ability to love hard-to-get-along-with in-laws. Take time to appreciate your wife's family—even if you have little in common with them. You both love the same woman—and that's enough common ground to make compromise (if necessary) worthwhile.

God, I pray for my wife's extended family. They are now a part of my family too. Help me to see their many assets and to set aside their faults. I pray for peace to prevail with all members of my family, including my biological family and hers. For certain ones, I pray for a softening of heart toward you and toward me. I pray for an end to any strife or misunderstanding. As I do what I can to live peaceably, Lord, I pray you will work in any potentially dangerous areas that are unknown to me. Create a deeper family bond, Lord, between me and my wife's family.

In Sickness and in Health

Gracious words are like a honeycomb,
sweetness to the soul and health to the body.
PROVERBS 16:24

Many of us stand before the pastor and vow to love our wife "in sickness and in health," all the while assuming that "health" will prevail over sickness. However, eventually one spouse of the couple will encounter sickness. At such times we must remember to stand by our wives as we know they would stand by us. Even if it's just a bad cold or the flu, be there for your wife.

Father, I pray for your protection regarding our health. I pray we'd recognize the habits that make for good health and incorporate them into our daily lives. I pray that sickness would never cause strife between us. When one of us becomes ill, give the other partner compassion and the ability to do what's necessary to restore health to the family. At such times, help me speak gracious words that bring sweetness to my wife's soul and health to her body.

GROWING OLD TOGETHER

*Even to your old age I am he, and
to gray hairs I will carry you.*
ISAIAH 46:4

Marriage is a journey a man and a woman take together for the rest of their lives. On that journey there are bumps in the road, unexpected changes of course, and often a roller-coaster of a ride. Growing old with the woman you love is a gift not all men experience. Cherish the gift…and no matter where you are in the journey now, relish the years you two will have together. Enjoy one another for the entire journey.

Lord, it's so easy for me to take your blessings for granted. The love my wife and I enjoy is an example. I don't pause often enough to thank you for her and the blessing she is in my life. I pray that we will be a couple who can enjoy many happy years together, even into our old age. At such a time, Father, you have said you will carry us. Thank you for this promise. Thank you for many years of sharing love with my wife.

A Husband's Words

Let no corrupting talk come out of your mouths,
but only such as is good for building up,
as fits the occasion, that it may
give grace to those who hear.
Ephesians 4:29

Words are powerful. They can hurt or heal, tear down or build up. A wife responds to the words of her husband, for good or for bad. She needs to hear from you that you consider her beautiful, that you cherish her, that she's a wonderful wife and life-mate. The amazing thing is that most women will evolve into what their husbands tell them they are. Build your wife up. Never ever tear her down with your words.

Lord, help me guard my mouth against saying harmful words to my wife. I pray that my words would only build her up, never tear her down. I pray to be a husband of grace, a man whose words bring healing to the hearer. Father, put a guard over my mouth when I'm about to speak unbecomingly to my wife. Instead, fill my mouth with words that edify.

The Listening Ear

[Make] your ear attentive to wisdom and
[incline] your heart to understanding.
Proverbs 2:2

When wives are asked what bugs them most about their husband, many respond, "He doesn't listen to me." Or they'll say, "He doesn't communicate with me. We have a silent marriage." God gave us two ears and one mouth—just perfect for listening twice as much as we speak.

When we fail to hear our wives, we're diminishing their worth. It's as if we're telling them, "What you have to say isn't important to me." Every good husband must also be a good listener. And sometimes that means *just* listening, not necessarily advising, counseling, or correcting. Just listen.

Father, I know that part of my calling as a husband is to listen to my wife. I pray for ears to better hear her—not just her words, but also her heart. I pray that I could truly tune my ears more attentively to her wisdom and incline my heart to the understanding she brings to our life together. Open my ears, Lord.

God Made Families

*Your wife will be like a fruitful
vine within your house;
your children will be like olive
shoots around your table.*
PSALM 128:3

The concept of family is God's idea, not man's. God ordains for men and women to fall in love, marry, carry out his work together, and raise godly children. Just so, the idea of you being called to be a husband to your wife requires careful attention to what God wants from you as a husband to your wife and a father to your children. Honor God's design for your family—and for your role as the head of the family.

Praise you, Lord, for inventing families. I thank you for my family and my calling to lead them into your destiny for us. I thank you for my wife's presence in our home and how her being there affects the very atmosphere of the house. I pray for the fruitfulness you have planned for us. I pray for our present children and for any additional "olive shoots" you send our way. May your blessing rest on our home.

Who Do You Hang With?

Iron sharpens iron, and one man sharpens another.
PROVERBS 27:17

Most men enjoy the company of other men. A guy's night out is as important as a gal's night out with other women. But who exactly are your companions? Do they aid you in becoming a better man? A better husband? Are the things you do together activities your wife would approve? Good men have a positive effect on one another—iron sharpening iron. Men whose activities skirt the edge of sin will ultimately lead to compromise. Choose good companions for friendship. Sharpen them, and allow them to sharpen you.

Thank you, God, for my male friends. I pray that we could grow closer as brothers in Christ and encouragers of one another. I pray you'll give me a sense of when we're veering off track and help us steady ourselves in you. I ask that you'll enable me to sense when a friend is going through a rough patch and needs my counsel or just my friendship. I pray for men in my life who will sharpen me like iron and whom I may also sharpen.

This Too Shall Pass

Teach us to number our days that
we may get a heart of wisdom.
PSALM 90:12

Life presents lots of good times…and lots of challenges too. Whatever is happening in your life and marriage right now—whether happy or sad—*it will pass*. A wise Christian man sets his roots on the firm rock of God's Word—which will never pass. Make sure your life and your marriage are firmly anchored on the Rock. All else shall eventually be only a memory.

Father God, teach me to number my days so that I may gain a heart of wisdom. All that's happening in my life now will pass soon enough and be replaced by new joys and sorrows. Help me, I pray, gain from my life experiences. Let nothing go to waste. Help me measure my life by your Word. Where my life doesn't align with Scripture, guide me into better alignment. Bless today my life and marriage—and all that pertains to me. I give you the glory.

Sowing and Reaping

Do not be deceived: God is not mocked,
for whatever one sows, that will he also reap.
GALATIANS 6:7

Anyone who's planted a garden knows that we will reap a harvest depending on the seeds we've sown. So too in marriage—we will reap what we sow. If we sow criticism, angry outbursts, or silence, we will reap the sad fruit of those seeds. On the other hand, if we sow kindness, encouragement, and praise, we will reap happiness in marriage. Sow good seed, add water, let the sun shine in, let time bring about a bountiful harvest.

God, I know that every day I plant seeds in my marriage. My words, attitudes, and actions will bring the inevitable crop...for good or for bad. Help me this day and always to plant seeds of love and service so that my wife and I will reap a good harvest—a rich and rewarding marriage. May we together sow spiritual seeds in each other's hearts; encouraging each other in the faith so that we reap a harvest of spiritual maturity.

Tell Her *Often*

Her children rise up and call her blessed;
her husband also, and he praises her:
"Many women have done excellently,
but you surpass them all."
PROVERBS 31:28-29

A wife needs to hear often the praises of her husband. For most men, this means a daily reminder to do so. Otherwise we get caught up in the activities of the day with words unsaid that need saying. In addition to verbal encouragement, consider sending an occasional card in the mail. Or leave her a love note where she's sure to find it. Do what you know she will appreciate. Do it often.

Father, I praise my wife as a Proverbs 31 woman. She has indeed done excellently, surpassing all. Help me remember to sing her praises to *her*, not just to you. Give me the right words that will make her day. Open my mind to specific ways I can bless her. Help me be creative in showing her my love for her. Most of all, thank you for choosing me to be her life-mate.

Sexual Compatibility

*Let marriage be held in honor among all,
and let the marriage bed be undefiled.*
Hebrews 13:4

In some marriages, the husband is more sexually inclined than the wife. Of course, that's not always the case. Sometimes wives complain about their husband's "dead battery." Sexual intimacy is by God's design and for the mutual enjoyment of both marriage partners. If either of you is out of sync with the other regarding sexual compatibility, you can begin by praying about it *together.* You can also see a good counselor. Too, there are also excellent books available, including *Intended for Pleasure* by Ed Wheat and *Red-Hot Monogamy* by Bill and Pam Farrel.

Keep in mind, though, that neither partner should ask the other to do something they're uncomfortable doing. That robs the partner of the joy of sexual intimacy.

Lord, thank you for the intimacy that is the ultimate physical expression of romantic love. I pray that my wife and I would each work toward complete sexual compatibility that leaves us both fulfilled. Remove from my life or my wife's life any impediments to our sexual happiness. May every aspect of our love, including sexual intimacy, be glorifying to you.

PRAYING TOGETHER

*Where two or three are gathered in my
name, there am I among them.*
MATTHEW 18:20

God brought you and your wife together. Your marriage was his doing. He will keep your love alive as you both keep him first in your marriage. One essential is praying together. If this has not been your practice, it can perhaps seem awkward at first…but do it anyway. Pray together out loud on a regular basis. Pray for each other, for your family, your finances, any other needs you might have. The old saying is still true: The couple that prays together stays together.

God, thank you for hearing my prayers. I praise you for all that my wife is to me, including her role as my prayer partner. I pray that you will be in our midst, according to your promise, as we pray to you. Give us a love for praying together that will withstand the many distractions that would keep us from prayer. Lead us, Father, through each day toward the destiny you have for us as a family. Hear our prayers, O Lord.

A Man of the Truth

*I rejoiced greatly when the brothers
came and testified to your truth,
as indeed you are walking in the truth.*

3 John 1:3

A good husband is a truth-teller. His wife trusts his words, and so do his kids. By being a man of the truth, a husband gains a reputation as a man of integrity—a *husband* of integrity. We become men of truth as we *walk* daily in truth. That is, we practice living by the truth every day.

God, I want to be a man of the truth, even when it's not convenient. I pray that I'll always speak the truth to my wife, that I will be a husband of integrity. Lord, teach me truth from your Word, help me implant divine truth in my heart so that my motives are based on truth, not presumption or falsehood. I pray that you'll help me discern truth and error when making decisions or evaluating people who are trying to influence me. Give me a sharp sense of right and wrong, Lord.

Forsaking All Others

Let not your heart turn aside
to [an adulteress's] ways;
do not stray into her paths.
Proverbs 7:25

When a spouse cheats on their mate, it's clear that the "forsaking all others" vow during the wedding ceremony wasn't truly meant. For a marriage to work, that one vow must be meant and must be kept. Casual attraction can lead to emotional affairs, and emotional affairs can lead to adultery. If you meant that vow of forsaking others, renew it now in your heart. If you've been eyeing someone other than your wife, cut it off now. Danger ahead!

Lord, I know some men have fallen prey to emotional affairs with women they meet. Some have even embarked on adulterous affairs as a result of seemingly innocent flirtations. I pray you'll send up a red flag in my mind if I ever show a sign of becoming interested (emotionally or otherwise) in any woman except my wife. I meant that vow I made on our wedding day. I renew that vow to remain true to my wife, always.

A Safe Man

In the fear of the Lord one has strong confidence,
and his children will have a refuge.
Proverbs 14:26

Every Christian man is called to be a "safe man." Safe for other women, safe for other men, safe for children. A safe man respects boundaries of others and is at heart a protector from unsafe men who prey on others. Most importantly, a safe man is also a safe husband to his wife.

Father, there are so many dangerous men running around committing evil acts against women, children, and even other men. This world needs a battalion of "safe men" who would never violate another person: man, woman, or child. Lord, I will be one of those safe men. Give me courage to be a protector for my family and for others who feel threatened by dangerous men. Help me to confront evil when I see it, whether sexual harassment, bullying, or emotional abuse. Lord, raise up other safe men who will protect the innocent.

May the fear of the Lord give us strong confidence against evil. May our children find refuge in safe men.

Prayer: Your Major Duty as a Husband

I tell you, whatever you ask in prayer,
believe that you have received
it, and it will be yours.
Mark 11:24

A husband has many responsibilities, but the most important is to bring his family before God in prayer. Intercession for our wives is paramount, but also praying for the welfare and the future of each of our children is just as important.

Dear Lord, I accept the role as primary intercessor for my family. I pray for my wife—for every aspect of her life, including her health, her spiritual life, her emotional well-being, and her relationship with me. Deepen our love and commitment, Lord. And for each of our children I ask that your hand be upon them. Grant them safety, give them a purpose in life, and create in them a heart that seeks hard after you.

HABITS

Do not be conformed to this world, but be transformed by the renewal of your mind, that by testing you may discern what is the will of God, what is good and acceptable and perfect.
ROMANS 12:2

Every man develops habits—some good, some not so good. As a husband, your habits can affect your wife. A Christian man is someone who is growing, maturing, and becoming more Christlike. As such, your bad habits need to fall away as they're replaced by good ones. Perhaps it's time to do an inventory. What bad habits can you put a stop to? What good habits should you be cultivating?

God, I realize a man's life is determined by his habits. You know my bad ones and my good ones. Help me replace the former with more of the latter. I pray for the transformation of my mind as I no longer conform to this world. I pray for a lifestyle that allows for the discerning of your good, acceptable, and perfect will. Establish in me, O Lord, the habits that will make for a fully realized Christian man.

The Beauty of Rest

*My presence will go with you, and
I will give you rest.*
Exodus 33:14

Christ is our spiritual "rest." In him we cease from striving for acceptance with God. When we live as rested men—men who trust fully in Christ—we are free to be the men and husbands we're meant to be. We can be authentic, transparent, generous men by nature. We can bring rest into our homes and to our wives. As we rest in Christ, we leave chaotic, frenzied thoughts and behaviors behind. In Christ, there is no frenzy.

Thank you, God, for rest! You provide rest physically when our bodies and minds are tired, and you provide spiritual rest in Jesus Christ. As I sometimes labor harder and longer than I should, remind me to slow down and rest. When I'm spiritually restless, I pray you'll remind me of your open invitation to rest in your presence. I thank you that I can bring a sense of rest and peace into my home as I myself enjoy your rest.

Your Wife's Emotions

A time to weep, and a time to laugh; a
time to mourn, and a time to dance.
ECCLESIASTES 3:4

Most women are more emotional than their husbands. A wise man will recognize the emotional needs of his wife and minister to those needs. Sometimes the need is simply to be held. Other times, your wife may want to talk out what's on her mind. At yet others, she may not know what she needs. A good husband will learn to sense the appropriate responses to his wife's emotional needs.

Thank you, Lord, for my wife's emotions. I know you designed emotions as an outlet for both genders. Help me, I pray, to discern the temporary and also the ongoing emotional needs of my wife. Show me how to help her work through those emotions. Guide us both as we learn to deal with each other's range of emotions.

LIKING WHAT SHE LIKES

*In humility count others more
significant than yourselves.*
PHILIPPIANS 2:3

What is your wife's favorite color? Her favorite flower? Her favorite restaurant? Would she rather go to the mountains or the beach? During your years of marriage, you as a husband will learn many things about your wife, much of which is new information since the wedding. You will have a lifetime to make your wife's preferences your own. Serving your wife often means forgoing your tastes for hers.

Dear God, I know a lot about my wife, but I need to learn more—both so I can please her and because I love her. Sometimes my own desires get in the way of learning about and fulfilling her desires. Help me set aside what I want and offer her what she wants. Help me truly count her as more significant than myself and my needs.

FORGIVING AND FORGETTING

Be kind to one another, tenderhearted,
forgiving one another,
as God in Christ forgave you.
EPHESIANS 4:32

Along the way in a marriage, there will be hurts and even sins against one another. When that happens, we can let the wound fester, or, if we're the offender, we can clear the air with a simple "I'm sorry." If we're the offended party, we can make a choice to drop our feelings of offense, regardless of whether our wife apologizes.

Once forgiven, an offense must be forgotten, just as God forgets the confessed sins of his children.

Remember this: A good marriage is the union of two forgivers.

Lord, I often miss the mark with my wife. I know my actions and my words sometimes cause hurt feelings or, worse, bitterness. Help me be kinder to my wife, more tenderhearted. Help me forgive her just as I want her to forgive me. Thank you that in Christ we both are forgiven for our sins. Help us display the forgiving spirit of Christ in our marriage.

Honoring God

Seek first the kingdom of God and his righteousness,
and all these things will be added to you.
Matthew 6:33

In the marriage relationship, you as the husband should think of putting your wife first. No other person on earth deserves your love more than the woman who has committed her life to loving you. But if both you and your wife will choose to put God first in your marriage, to honor him in all you do, you'll find that God, in return, will bless your union. You can't out-give God.

Father, I thank you for placing, in my heart, a hunger for you. I pray that I'll always put my wife first as the one person on this planet whom I love and honor the most. She knows, however, that ultimately you are the one who has first place in my heart. Lord, I seek after you, and in so doing, I know you'll impart added blessings to my life. Seeking you first makes me a better husband. I praise you, Lord, for you are worthy!

Mutual Submission

[Submit] to one another out of reverence for Christ.
Ephesians 5:21

Submission has gotten a bad rap. Instead of seeing submission as knuckling under to someone with bully-like force, we need to see it as a positive attribute in our wives as well as in ourselves as we learn to mutually respond in submission, as Ephesians 5:21 exhorts us to do.

God, teach me about submission. Show me how to enjoy mutual submission with those in my circle. And with my wife, help me to submit to her advice and even correction when I need to, just as she will submit to me when appropriate. Keep us both openhearted and openhanded enough to submit without feeling like we're being lorded over. Let there never be even a hint of bullying or domineering on my part. Bring us into the right understanding of mutual submission—both in our marriage and with our brothers and sisters in Christ.

THE STORMS OF LIFE

He made the storm be still, and the
waves of the sea were hushed.
PSALM 107:29

The time to prepare for storms is before they hit. That's true in the natural sense, and also true of marriages. You *will* face storms in your marriage relationship. Some will be mild tempests that blow over quickly. A few may be tornado-strength, with all the accompanying damage. So how will you and your wife handle these approaching storms? Praying together helps. Renewing your ongoing life commitment to each other is a must. Learning from other couples can be useful. A good marriage can last any storm if the couple stays prepared. Don't wait until the clouds turn dark. That may be too late.

Dear Lord, you are the one who brings my wife and me through the storms of life. Help us become more securely anchored in your love. May we trust more fully in you when we see storm clouds approaching. Bring us through each gale-force wind with renewed strength in our marriage. May every storm be followed by sunny days and renewed commitment to each other.

41

HOUSEHOLD DUTIES

*She rises while it is yet night and provides food
for her household and portions for her maidens.*
PROVERBS 31:15

There's no rule book that says household chores are "women's work." The truth is that running a household is labor- and time-intensive. The old proverb "many hands make light work" applies here. Both husbands and wives should share the household chores, divvying them up according to the abilities and preferences of each partner. Pull together as a couple. Work with each other. Do your part, men.

Dear God, overseeing a household is hard work. First, I give thanks that we have a home to take care of. I thank you for every task involved in keeping a household operating smoothly, even the seemingly minor tasks. Remind me when I forget to pitch in and do my part. Help me see what needs to be done so my wife doesn't have to ask me to help. Show me the jobs that should fall to me, not my wife. Grant me joy as I serve my family by doing my share of the household chores.

A Husband's Kiss

Let him kiss me with the kisses of his mouth!
For your love is better than wine.
Song of Solomon 1:2

After holding hands, a kiss is often the next step to a couple's intimacy. After the wedding, as time passes, kisses can become routine—the light touching of lips in the morning as you each go about your day… or the last "goodnight" as the bedroom light is turned off. But kisses should always remain more than a slight token of affection. They must never become routine. A husband's kiss tells his wife he still loves her with the intensity he felt on their wedding day. It tells her she is the focus of his love. The touch of a kiss is more significant than most husbands realize.

God, may I never take the giving of my affection to my wife for granted. I pray that every kiss I give will be a reminder to my wife of my love for her. May she know the depth of my love for her through the affection I show her. May my kisses be as meaningful now as they were on the day we were married.

LEARNING HER WEAKNESSES

My grace is sufficient for you, for my
power is made perfect in weakness.
2 CORINTHIANS 12:9

Not long after the wedding, the bride and groom begin to learn about their partner's weaknesses. The inability or unwillingness to deal with a spouse's weaknesses can ruin a marriage. Don't go looking for weaknesses in your spouse, but when you do spot one, *do not criticize or complain.* Don't offer advice or correction. Instead, gently accept your wife's weaknesses in the same way you want her to accept yours. If she asks for help, give it. But even then, be patient and appreciate her for her many strengths.

God, when I consider my weaknesses, it makes it easier to accept weaknesses in other people. My wife has many great qualities, but she also has weaknesses unique to her. Lord, I pray you'll help me keep silent about her weak points unless she brings them up. And when she does talk about her weaknesses, help me to help her past them. I pray, too, for my wife to be patient with me in light of my weaknesses. May both of us experience your power made perfect in our weaknesses.

A Husband's Touch

His left hand is under my head, and
his right hand embraces me!
SONG OF SOLOMON 2:6

Your wife is standing at the stove or folding laundry or paying bills as you walk by. What do you do? You gently touch her on the arm or back. You might say something, or you might just let the gentle touch speak for you. For many women (and men too), one of their love languages is touch. But if a husband doesn't know this about his wife, he won't give her the affectionate touch that she finds affirming. Learn to speak love to your wife through gentle touch. You will be rewarded.

Lord, I know that one of my wife's love languages is touch. I pray you'll remind me to not just casually walk by her or take her presence for granted, but to use the power of touch to reaffirm my love for her. May I also be sensitive to when touching her is not her desired love language.

Praying for Your Wife

*[Pray] at all times in the Spirit, with
all prayer and supplication.*
Ephesians 6:18

It's through your prayers that you can bless your wife and see her overcome obstacles in her life or work. Take time to step away from your routine every day and pray briefly for your wife. Learn her needs by simply asking her how you can pray for her. Let her know she's at the top of your prayer list. You are the most important intercessor in her life.

Lord, I intercede for my wife today. I thank you for her presence in my life. Thank you for allowing her to love me and want me as her life companion. I pray for her needs, both the ones I know and the ones I don't know. I pray for her walk with you, Father. Strengthen her spiritually, emotionally, and physically. Bring blessing into her life, Lord, and as much as possible, bring that blessing through me.

Her Nesting Instinct

Even the sparrow finds a home,
and the swallow a nest for herself,
where she may lay her young,
at your altars, O LORD of hosts,
my King and my God.
Blessed are those who dwell in your house,
ever singing your praise! Selah.
PSALM 84:3-4

For many wives, their home is the place where they can "nest." Make sure your wife knows she has the freedom to create the nest she wants. If she asks your advice, offer it...but defer to her wishes as often as you can. Never just say, "It doesn't matter to me what you decide." Instead, let her know you value her taste and will honor her decisions. Show interest, and make sure her desires are respected.

Dear God, thank you for my wife's desire to make our home a comfortable welcoming place. I pray you'll give her creative ideas for our nest and that I'll give her the freedom to implement those ideas. I pray specifically for our home—that your peace always be felt in it, and that your blessing would rest on it.

GETTING HELP
WHEN NECESSARY

The way of a fool is right in his own
eyes, but a wise man listens to advice.
PROVERBS 12:15

Men are sometimes seen as stubborn when it comes to getting outside help. Some put off going to the doctor when they know they should. Some won't even consult a road map when lost. And when it comes to their marriage—a major aspect of a man's life—some husbands refuse to go with their wives for counseling when necessary. Don't make this mistake. A good Christian counselor can help iron out small problems before they become big. Be willing to have a third ear listen in on your marriage.

Lord, thank you for my marriage. When it's going well, I rejoice in the smooth sailing we both enjoy. But when the waters become rough, may we look to you to calm any rough seas we encounter. Then, Lord, we trust you to bring good counselors our way if necessary. I pray that neither of us would balk at seeking help when we need it. A wise sailor on rough seas will look to the experienced captain for instructions on arriving at port safely.

YOUR CHILDREN'S RESPECT

*Husbands, love your wives, and
do not be harsh with them.*
COLOSSIANS 3:19

One of a parent's duties is to instill respect for elders—and particularly parents—in their children. A dad promotes respect for mom in the eyes of the children by showing respect himself. Your kids have big eyes and listening ears. The way you speak and act toward your wife will be mimicked by them as they grow older. When disrespect is shown to your wife by your children, correct them, and then ask yourself if they were parroting what they've heard from you.

Lord, I pray that you would calm me down when I'm tempted to be harsh or to show disrespect to my wife. Help me remember that others see, hear, or even sense my attitude toward her, for good or for bad. When the words about to come out of my mouth are inappropriate, I pray you'll prompt me to silence instead of allowing me to show disrespect. Help me to find words to honor my wife in front of all who might hear.

READING THE WORD

All Scripture is breathed out by God and
profitable for teaching, for reproof,
for correction, and for training in righteousness,
that the man of God may be complete,
equipped for every good work.
2 TIMOTHY 3:16-17

A Christian husband's manual for life is his Bible. In its pages, he learns how to be a better man, husband, and father. The Bible is also the manual for a great marriage, best evidenced as a man and wife read from the Word of God together daily. Even if it's just five minutes a day, take time with your wife to read from Psalms, the Gospels, Galatians, Ephesians, or other books in the Scriptures. Grow together in God's Word.

Father, thank you for your Word. I pray that it would speak to my wife and me as a couple. From its pages, please guide us, correct us, and comfort us. Remind us to make time daily to get into the Bible. By the power of the Holy Spirit, teach us how to live. Teach us how to serve one another. Teach us how to be a godly and happy couple. May your Word reprove, correct, and train us in righteousness.

MAKING A ROUTINE
DAY SPECIAL

Enjoy life with the wife whom you love.
ECCLESIASTES 9:9

A wise husband sends his wife a card, flowers, or candy on their anniversary, Valentine's Day, her birthday, and other important dates. But a wiser husband also surprises his wife on routine days when it is least expected. In doing so, you let your wife know you're thinking of her all the time.

God, I know that every day with my wife is a special day. In that sense, every day is Valentine's Day. Help me not just to remember her on special occasions, but prompt me to go the extra mile and remember her when she least expects it. It will be a reminder that my love for her is constant, even on ordinary days.

Thankfulness to God

[Give] thanks always and for everything to God
the Father in the name of our Lord Jesus Christ.
Ephesians 5:20

Give thanks for your wife. Remember how God brought her to you. Think about the time when you first realized she was the one. Offer praise to God for this amazing gift he has given you. Oh, sure, there may be days when you wonder why you ever gave up the single life for marriage, but those days are quickly forgotten as you give thanks for the woman God chose to be your bride.

Today, Lord, I offer praise for my wonderful wife. How you brought us together is amazing. Yes, you orchestrated the whole thing—and are still conducting the symphony of our marriage. Thank you for the music we make together. Thank you for the love we share. Thank you for the future you're unveiling for us day by day. Praise you, Father!

BEST FRIENDS

A friend loves at all times.
PROVERBS 17:17

In a lifetime, friends come and go. But if we allow our wife to be our best friend in addition to being our lifetime lover, we will have a best friend who will stick with us through thick and thin. Learn to think of your wife in terms of friendship as well as romance. Treasure this friendship as the most intimate you'll ever have.

God, I love the hymn "What a Friend We Have in Jesus," and I also want to acknowledge what a friend I have in my wife. May I today and always be committed to her as my best friend in life. I pray you will give us the kind of friendship through our marriage that others notice with admiration. Father, do whatever is necessary to deepen our friendship. May we both love the other "at all times."

Her Life's Goals

I can do all things through him who strengthens me.
Philippians 4:13

Women, like most men, have certain life goals. Do you know your wife's goals? How can you help her meet those goals? If she has a hard time naming her goals, you can help there too by asking her some relevant questions. Be in your wife's corner all the way. Take a genuine interest in supporting her. Help her be the best she can be.

God, my wife has so many great talents. As her husband, help me be her encourager and confidence-builder. Show me ways to affirm her talents and help her be all she can be. Lord, give her favor in the eyes of others who can help her. Bless her in all that she does, dear God.

"You Will Be My Witnesses"

*You will receive power when the Holy Spirit
has come upon you, and you will be my
witnesses in Jerusalem and in all Judea and
Samaria, and to the end of the earth.*

Acts 1:8

Christians are to be witnesses to a Christless world.
Your marriage is a part of that witness. You and
your wife can have the kind of marriage in which other
couples can see Christ manifest. In that sense, you and
your wife are on display to the non-Christian couples
you know. Be a light in a dark world. Show the happiness that love and commitment bring. Be a witness in
your marriage.

Lord, my wife and I know some other couples who
need to know you. I pray that our marriage would be
a witness to these men and women and that in some
way we can show them the importance of placing you
at the center of their marriage. I pray too that you will
bring other couples our way who need to know you.
Strengthen our witness, Lord. May we become an
oasis for struggling couples who need help.

LEARNING TO LAUGH TOGETHER

A joyful heart is good medicine, but a
crushed spirit dries up the bones.
PROVERBS 17:22

There's an old saying that if you want to make God laugh, tell him your plans. That begs the question: Does God laugh? The Old Testament portrays him as laughing at those who would attempt to thwart his will.

I'm convinced God does have a sense of humor. I'm also convinced that every couple can benefit from the humor that marriage inevitably brings. Sometimes, though, we need to look for the humor in what might otherwise be a dark situation. Nevertheless, the end result of a good laugh is worth the search. Bring humor into your marriage when you can. It's the best medicine.

Praise you, Lord, for the gift of laughter. Help me and my wife see the humor in our marriage and even in our occasional problem. Spare us from the dryness of bones that come from a crushed spirit. May our home be known as a beacon of humor and laughter. May the medicine of a joyful heart be ours today and always.

Dealing with Anger

Let all bitterness and wrath and anger and
clamor and slander be put away from you,
along with all malice.
Ephesians 4:31

We all get angry at times. That's understandable. What's not understandable is anger directed at our wife, especially if the anger turns violent. Sadly, Christian men are not immune to perpetrating abuse. It's reported that 25 percent of Christian homes witness abuse of some kind. That means roughly one in four men reading this right now may abuse their wife or their children. That must not continue. Men are to be safeguards for their family. Protectors.

Yes, you *will* get angry. Ask God to show you how to safely defuse your anger. Don't let your wife bear the brunt of your bad temper.

God, I'm amazed when I hear of Christian husbands who in any way abuse their wife or children. Such abuse is sin against them and against you. I pray you'll help me refrain from any abusive activity toward my wife and children. Show me ways to defuse my anger when triggered by some unexpected event. Teach me how to be a healer and protector of my family.

A MARATHON, NOT A SPRINT

Do you not know that in a race all the runners
run, but only one receives the prize?
So run that you may obtain it.
1 CORINTHIANS 9:24

When we're first married, we're excited about our new status. Our love is fresh and our manner gentle. That youthful energy is good for a sprint, but marriage is a marathon. It requires pacing yourself, looking ahead to the goal, and running effectively. Never allow bumps in the road to end the race for you. If you fall, get back up. Run with the marital energy God supplies. Reach for the finish-line tape of a marriage well-lived.

Lord, my wife and I are in the marathon of marriage. Sometimes we need you to supply a second wind. We need you to show us how to pace ourselves. We need to see the promised finish line ahead of us and pursue it with joy. Father, give us the energy we need to run the race well and to end well.

Modeling Love in Front
of Your Children

*Train up a child in the way he should go; even
when he is old he will not depart from it.*
PROVERBS 22:6

If you want your children to grow up as mature, responsible Christians and live happy, productive lives, that's what you must model for them. Make sure your kids see you and your wife kiss often (if they giggle at you, they're getting it!). Make sure they overhear you praise your wife. Make sure they observe you helping in the kitchen or with the laundry. Include them in a good family hug often. Model love.

God, sometimes it scares me that my kids look to me as a model man and husband. My sons will likely become husbands like me. My daughters will seek husbands like me—if I'm the godly husband you've called me to be. Lord, help me model a husband and father's love in all that I do. Open my kids' eyes to the things I do right. Help them look away when I mess up. Bring about a happy future for my kids because of what they see in me.

More Time

Let your fountain be blessed,
and rejoice in the wife of your youth.
Proverbs 5:18

You have only so many years, days, hours, minutes, and seconds on this planet. When the sand runs out of your hourglass, it will be too late to do things differently. The time for living a happy marriage is *now.* Take time with your wife. Relish each day with her. Thank God for the time you two have left together. Make the most of each day.

God, my time is in your hands. You have my life mapped out—my years on this earth are determined by you. I pray I would be a good steward of my time. May I live a life with few regrets—especially about my marriage. Lord, now is the time for me to be the good husband my wife needs. Now is the time I need to man up to my responsibilities. Now is the time for which you have called me to be faithful. Help me, Lord.

STRENGTH DURING ADVERSITY

If you faint in the day of adversity,
your strength is small.
PROVERBS 24:10

It's hard to remain standing during adversity if you're alone. But you have a partner—an encourager during adversity. Normally one plus one equals two. But when the ones are a husband and a wife, the effect is more than doubled. Adversity tests your strength as a couple, and in so doing, it can make you stronger if you count on each other...and God.

Lord, you have total control over what happens to us. Our past, present, and future belong to you. There will likely be some troubling times ahead, as there are for most couples. Lord, you have given us each other for those times. With each other, our strength is more than doubled and we can make it past the adversity—we can even see it become a blessing. Thank you, Lord, for the gift of each other—and for the gift of your presence throughout our journey together.

Saying No to Divorce

He said to them, "Because of your hardness
of heart Moses allowed you to divorce your
wives, but from the beginning it was not so."
Matthew 19:8-9

Jesus noted that the reason for divorce was hardness of heart. That is, one member of the couple has allowed their heart to grow hard as the two grew apart for one reason or another. This begs for a simple alternative to divorce: the softening of the heart. Divorce need not be. Reconcile your differences and your marriage. Own up to your marital sins and shortcomings, and pledge to become the husband your wife needs as she pledges to become the wife you need. Say no to divorce by saying yes to a softened heart.

Lord, soften our hearts! Whenever circumstances or trials tend toward hardening our hearts, I pray we would not allow that hardening to happen. Keep our hearts tender and open to each other. Draw us closer through every trial and every joy. Remove any obstacles to a soft heart. Create in each of us a compassion for the other, and may we never allow our hearts to become hard.

WATCHING OUT FOR PRIDE

*One's pride will bring him low, but he who
is lowly in spirit will obtain honor.*
PROVERBS 29:23

The husband, as servant-leader of his family, can be tempted to be prideful if he's not careful. The wise man knows that blessing comes from God, and any success he has in leading his family is due to God's work within him and his family. Willful pride harms a family, especially the children, who are likely to rebel as their own pride eventually clashes with Dad's. Stay humble, and watch your family flourish under your leadership.

God, nobody knows more than me how much I must depend on you as I lead my family and as I become the husband my wife needs. Keep me from pride, Lord, even if a humbling experience becomes necessary. May my pride not become a stumbling block for my wife or my children. May I be lowly in spirit rather than brought low by foolish pride. Once again, I renew my dependence on you, Lord.

The Little Things

*One who is faithful in a very little
is also faithful in much.*
LUKE 16:10

It's the little things that can determine whether a marriage will be successful or fail. On the one hand, doing small kindnesses for your wife reminds her that you're thinking of her. On the other, small slights toward your wife reinforce your thoughtlessness. Make a note on your calendar to look for some small thing to do to please your wife. Flowers, candy, a love note, a back rub, washing the dishes, dinner out—whatever small thing you know that pleases her, do it often.

God, help me be a faithful man in not just big things, but in the little things too. Give me eyes to see what I may not have seen before—small jobs around the house or kindnesses that I've overlooked. May the many little things I do faithfully add up to one big thing: a happy wife.

CARING FOR YOUR WIFE

Let each of you look not only to his own interests,
but also to the interests of others.
PHILIPPIANS 2:4

We husbands often forget how to care for our wives. They're not self-maintained—at least not in the romance department. We take care of our cars, we tend to our jobs, we invest in our hobbies…yet we often forget to care for our wife as our partner in life. But love does that. Love cares for the one who is loved. Consider a new way to show your wife how much you care for her.

Father, I need to give more care and attention to my wife. She means so much to me. Help me show her how I value her in my life by finding additional ways to care for her, realizing how often she shows how much she cares for me. As I care for her, may it serve to increase my love for her—and her love for me.

WORRY AND STRESS

[Cast] all your anxieties on him,
because he cares for you.
1 PETER 5:7

What are you worried about? What stresses you? A stressed man is a lesser husband. His focus on his wife is necessarily weakened as he musters the strength to deal with the cause of his stress. For this reason, a husband's spiritual strength must remain vital. He must learn to immediately shift incoming burdens into the Lord's hands. Let God care for you and your problems. Let him offer counsel—and that counsel will sometimes come through your wife. Let her in on your concerns too. Many a wise wife has become her husband's problem solver.

Lord, I cast all my cares and anxieties on you. Take them, for they are too heavy for me. Thank you for the many times you've spoken to me through wise words from my wife and given her the answer that I seek. Father, give me ears to hear when she counsels me. May she become your megaphone to reach my dull ears. Thank you for your care for both of us, especially through anxious times.

The Danger of Passivity

Do not be slothful in zeal, be fervent
in spirit, serve the Lord.
ROMANS 12:11

In today's culture, there is sometimes a tendency to emasculate men, rendering them passive. Most wives, however, prefer a husband who is appropriately proactive. A man who takes the lead in serving, protecting, honoring, and looking out for his family. When a husband is too passive, the wife reluctantly steps in and assumes a role that would better be filled by the husband. Learn how to be a husband who is tenderly looking for opportunities to lead his family.

God, help me be a man of action for my family. Guide me as I take the initiative in leading my wife. Help me to be the kind of leader a wife is eager to follow, not reluctant and unsure of where he's leading. Lord, I don't want to be the passive kind of man who simply lets things happen. I want to be the kind of family leader who shows the way ahead with confidence, even as I do so with a prayer on my lips. Thank you, God, for the privilege of being a servant-leader to my family.

CHERISH HER

*Husbands, love your wives, as
Christ loved the church
and gave himself up for her.*
EPHESIANS 5:25

When wives are asked how they want to be treated by their husbands, many respond that they want to be *cherished*. Webster defines *cherish* as "to hold dear; to feel or show affection for." It can mean to consider the cherished one as "special" or "prized." Keep the word *cherish* close to your heart. This is what your wife wants from you.

God, how I do cherish my wife! You chose her out of millions of women to be my companion for life. I pray I can be the cherishing husband she needs. I pray she daily feels loved and prized by me. I pray I never let her feel common or less than praiseworthy. Lord, keep the word *cherish* in my mind each day.

DITCH THE PORN

I will set no wicked thing before mine eyes.
PSALM 101:3 (KJV)

A survey by the respected Barna Group revealed that among married Christian men, 55 percent look at pornography at least monthly. We men are aroused visually; thus temptation can be found in what we put before our eyes. Not only does porn tempt us to evil, it insults our wives, does harm to our marriage, and weakens us spiritually.

If porn is a problem for you, get help. Online porn can be blocked through available apps. An accountability partner from your church may also help. Do what it takes to ditch the porn before it assaults your marriage—possibly fatally.

God, I vow to "set no wicked thing before mine eyes." Purify my heart, O Lord. Keep my mind focused on wholesome thoughts as I firmly reject temptations to lust or seek out pornographic images. Strengthen me spiritually, God, for the spirit is truly willing, but the flesh is often weak. If necessary, Lord, lead me to other men with whom I can be an active accountability partner. If need be, I will sign up for accountability software for my computer. Whatever it takes, Lord.

UNDERSTANDING HER GIFTS

We are his workmanship, created
in Christ Jesus for good works,
which God prepared beforehand, that
we should walk in them.

EPHESIANS 2:10

Your wife is gifted in ways you are not. Recognize her gifts and celebrate them. Never squelch your wife's talents…especially when they're talents you truly need. Give your wife every opportunity to use her gifts to the maximum. Find ways to celebrate her achievements. Thank God daily for the ways he has gifted your wife.

Dear Lord, I see my wife as a demonstration of your workmanship. I know she was created for good works that you prepared before she was even born. Now, Lord, she walks in those works and brings them to pass—all through the power of your Holy Spirit working in her. Today, Father, I intercede for my wife and her many gifts. Use her to the limit, Lord. Fulfill your plan for her in its entirety. Lead me as I do my part to encourage and support her as she lives out your plan.

SURPRISE! MEN AND WOMEN ARE DIFFERENT

God created man in his own image, in
the image of God he created him;
male and female he created them.
GENESIS 1:27

How ingenious of God to make men and women so different from each other. The reason, of course, is that we're to complement each other. Just as we're opposite physically so that we can fit together and become one in intercourse, so too are we meant to put both of our different halves together to become one better unit. Sometimes our differences become a cause of conflict. "Why can't she be more like me?" we ask. But we really don't want that. Then there would be two halves just the same, not complementary.

Thank God for the differences between you and your wife.

God, your design for two human genders is truly remarkable! I thank you for creating me as a man and my wife as a woman and that we complement each other very well. The fact that we're also created in your image is even more astounding. Lord, may we both reflect to others your image being conformed in us by the Holy Spirit.

Is Marriage a 50/50 Proposition?

I will betroth you to me forever. I will betroth you to me in righteousness and in justice, in steadfast love and in mercy. I will betroth you to me in faithfulness. And you shall know the LORD.

HOSEA 2:19-20

Any husband who thinks he contributes 50 percent of himself to the marriage and his wife does the same is in for a disappointment. Marriage is never 50/50. It's 100/100. Both husband and wife must be all-in for the marriage to work best. Don't hold back in marriage. If you want any enterprise to succeed, you give it your all. How much more so in marriage—the most important investment in your life.

Lord, I give my all to my wife and our marriage. I give 100 percent, nothing held back. You have been an example of total commitment in saving me and my wife. You gave—and still give—100 percent of yourself to each of us as we walk in the power of the Holy Spirit. Father, help us stay 100-percenters for the rest of our lives.

Your Wife Won't Complete You

You are complete in Him, who is the
head of all principality and power.
Colossians 2:10 (NKJV)

A wife complements her husband, but she doesn't complete him. A man is a man on his own—and with God's power working within him. As you and your wife each look to God to empower you and to complete you, you can better complement, but not complete, each other.

God, I thank you for establishing me as "complete" in Christ. Most days I don't feel that way, yet I know it is so. I am "in Him," and from him I grow as a Christian and as a man. I pray you'll be with me as I man up to my responsibilities. Show me how to better serve you and my wife. Help both of us discern the ways in which we complement one another. Thank you for your power working within us.

Manning Up

Be watchful, stand firm in the
faith, act like men, be strong.
1 Corinthians 16:13-14

Someone has said, "The only difference between a boy and a man is the cost of his toys." As men, it's time to put the toys aside and man up to our responsibilities. Whether at work or as men of God in our local church or as husbands, it's time to be fully men. This means accepting, not evading responsibility. It means doing, not just talking. It means working, not just playing. It means being a husband to your wife, not a little boy in a man's body.

Lord, I want to be like King David—a man after your own heart. Help me in my spiritual life as I man up to my Christian responsibilities. Help me to man up as a husband. Set my heart free from any childish "toys" that rob me of time with my family. Give me a more complete vision of how you see me as a man—and help me aim my life toward that vision.

RESPECT

*There is neither Jew nor Greek, there
is neither slave nor free,
there is no male and female, for you
are all one in Christ Jesus.*
GALATIANS 3:28

Men rightly want their wives to respect them. But husbands must also respect their wives. *Respect*, in this case, means seeing each other as equals in every imaginable way. Though men and women have different roles as defined by God, neither is inferior to the other. Smart husbands recognize the life and work of God in their wives and give them due respect.

Dear Lord, my wife and I are the same in your eyes. There is no male or female. And yet we do have different duties as outlined in your Word. Neither role—husband or wife—is better than the other...they're just different. Help me as I show respect to my wife as she lives out her God-designed role in life. Allow me to contribute to her happiness as much as I can. Remind me always to show her the respect due her. Thank you, Lord.

LEAVE THE PAST IN THE PAST

I am he who blots out your
transgressions for my own sake,
and I will not remember your sins.
ISAIAH 43:25

One way to fail a marriage is to carry mistakes from the past into the marriage relationship. You've made mistakes in your past—possibly very serious ones. Sins, even. Perhaps your wife made similar mistakes—yes, sins even. But now that you are Christians, those confessed and forsaken sins are so far gone that even God doesn't remember them. Why, then, should you? Why should your wife remember them? It's foolish to allow the regrets of the past to destroy what should be a fantastic future. Leave the past in the past.

God, it amazes me that you have chosen to entirely forget my many sins. For that reason, there's no room for my past to affect my present or my future. I pray, then, that I could truly forget my past mistakes and move ahead as a clean, forgiven, godly man. Because of your grace, I can live free from the past...and so can my wife.

GREAT EXPECTATIONS

The hope of the righteous brings joy,
but the expectation of the wicked will perish.
PROVERBS 10:28

Both bride and groom enter a marriage with certain expectations of how life will be. Some of those expectations are too high and unrealistic. Others may be too low—particularly if you weigh your marriage against your parents' union, whether for good or bad. This is *your* life and *your* marriage. Don't let expectations—too high or too low—rob you of what God has for your marriage.

Father God, I believe you have a specific plan for my wife and me. Our marriage is a fulfillment of your will for each of us. Help us both to not compare ourselves or our marriage to those of others, especially not that of our parents. This life is ours to live. The joy you have for us cannot be compared to the joys of other couples. Give us realistic expectations so that we will be satisfied with our lot, never disappointed in your plan for us.

What If…?

*Let not your hearts be troubled. Believe
in God; believe also in me.*
John 14:1

There are two two-word laments that can destroy a life—and a marriage. The first lament refers to the past and is "If only…" As in, "If only I hadn't committed that sinful act." The other lament is more often about the future and is "What if…?" As in, "What if I lose my job?" Or "What if my wife no longer loves me?" Either lament is deadly and is definitely not the voice of God. Any such laments about your marriage or your life must be rejected immediately. If not, you may needlessly dwell on them and cause undue stress. God is not in the "If only…" or "What if…?" business. Neither must we be.

Lord, when my heart is troubled over "What if…?" or "If only…," comfort me by reminding me that any statement beginning with those words is not a statement of faith. Fill me, Lord, with the kind of faith that rejects worry about the past or future. Help me as I truly believe in you and your plan for our lives.

FULLY PRESENT

*Complete my joy by being of the same
mind, having the same love,
being in full accord and of one mind.*
PHILIPPIANS 2:2

Life is full of distractions. Work, politics, finances,
health issues—all these and more vie for our attention. Sometimes when our wives need our attention,
we don't remove ourselves from our present distraction
to be fully present for them. We might respond, "Yes,
dear" without even realizing what was said.

When you are with your wife, give her your full
attention. *Be* there. Fully present.

Lord, I'm so easily distracted. Sometimes without
meaning to, I tune my wife out. She speaks, but I don't
hear. In a sense, when I'm distracted, I'm not really
there for her. Open my eyes and ears, Lord. Help me
to turn away from what I'm doing and be fully present
for her. After all, when we pray, we want you to be fully
present with us...and you are.

"THANK YOU"

*I thank my God always when I
remember you in my prayers.*
PHILEMON 4

Marriage can become literally thankless if you forget the appropriate responses to your wife's many kindnesses toward you. A good meal always deserves a thank you. If she's the laundry person in the house, a thank you for that chore is also in order (though laundry is one chore you might consider undertaking in a busy household). Being thankful to your wife—and making sure she knows you're thankful—contributes to a happy wife.

God, create in me a thankful spirit. Help me notice the many tasks and kindnesses my wife does that I might easily overlook. With your help, I will also demonstrate the principle of thankfulness to our children. First, thankfulness to you for all you are and all you do. Then thankfulness to my wife and the mother of my children.

THE BIG DECISIONS

*Let the wise hear and increase in learning, and
the one who understands obtain guidance.*
PROVERBS 1:5

Who makes the big decisions in your home? A wise husband never decides important matters without seriously considering his wife's input. While many men make decisions based on the available information, a wife can bring the added bonus of simply sensing the rightness or wrongness of a major change. Give her time to completely express her opinions. The blend of your deliberations with her additional insight can save you from potential disaster. Never make a move against your wife's better judgment.

God, you've given me a great counselor in my wife. I pray for you to continue to minister wisdom to me through her words. Increase her insightfulness as you increase my ability to receive good counsel from her. When the big decisions face us, give us unity in how we choose to proceed. May we never act hastily when it comes to making a decision. Instead, may we wait for clarity and agreement between us.

DEALING WITH SIN

The wages of sin is death, but the free gift of
God is eternal life in Christ Jesus our Lord.
ROMANS 6:23

All have sinned. Every husband on the planet has had to deal with his sin. Christians, of course, have forgiveness of sin through the shed blood of Christ. Unfortunately, that doesn't mean that we always deal with our sin as we should (repent, confess, walk forward in forgiveness). We may in fact continue with sinful patterns in one or more areas of our life. Doing so is harmful to us and to our marriage. If you're aware of ongoing sin in your life, for your own good, forsake it now. Receive forgiveness and the power to move ahead, free from that sin.

Lord, you know the traps that easily ensnare me. Temptations of the flesh or unreasonable ambitions or covetousness—the desire to be something or someone I'm not. All these and more can take me off the path. Father, when these things happen, may I come to you as the prodigal, asking for forgiveness and a fresh start. Renew me with your power and strength.

SECOND WIND

Behold, I am doing a new thing; now it
springs forth, do you not perceive it?
I will make a way in the wilderness
and rivers in the desert.

ISAIAH 43:19

The great thing about our Christian faith is that it brings new life and restoration to troubled lives. No matter if the situation is small or large, God can restore us, redeem us, make us as good as new. At some point, most every marriage needs to experience a second wind. May the gentle breeze of God's second wind blow into your marriage.

Dear Lord, I pray for the fresh breeze of a second wind on our marriage. As time goes by, may our love and commitment to each other deepen in ways we hadn't even considered. Give us a renewed sense of what true love is—the act of giving sacrificially to the other. Thank you that when we find ourselves in the wilderness, you make a way. You bring forth rivers in the desert. I praise you for those flowing rivers.

GENEROSITY

Give, and it will be given to you. Good measure,
pressed down, shaken together, running over,
will be put into your lap. For with the measure
you use it will be measured back to you.
LUKE 6:38

Some of us are naturally generous. Others of us need to learn to be generous. Generous to those in need, to our families, and to our wives. Generous with time, money, our bodies, every part of us. Your wife, in a very real sense, "owns" you. Be generous in giving her what is rightfully hers.

God, I pray that my wife and I would continually learn to be good givers. Instill in us a generous spirit and enable us to give more than we give now—both financially and of ourselves. I praise you that no matter how generous we are, we can never rival your generosity. Thank you for providing for us the way you do. May we be channels of blessings as you work through us to help others.

House Blessings

Peace be within your walls and
security within your towers!
PSALM 122:7

God intends for your home to be a place of blessing. He wants his peace to prevail in your house. As head of the house, it's your privilege to pray over your home and confirm God's blessing on it and all who live there. May your home be *blessed.*

God, thank you for the family you've given me to lead and the home in which we live. I pray a blessing over our house and each family member. May your peace be within our walls and prevail in all we do. Keep strife far away from us. Guard us from disaster and danger. Be our source of security in dangerous times. May your glory be felt in our home by all who enter.

Healthy Boundaries

You have fixed all the boundaries of the earth; you have made summer and winter.
Psalm 74:17

Love between a husband and wife is not without boundaries. The respect of another person means respecting certain boundaries. Bathroom privacy is one example. No name-calling. No speaking ill of your spouse to outsiders. No raising of voices in anger. Certainly no abuse of any kind. What are your marital boundaries? Stick to them.

God, you fixed the boundaries of the earth. You have fixed the times and seasons. Just as there are physical boundaries and seasonal boundaries for good reason, so too are there relational boundaries, even between a husband and wife.

I need to know and respect my wife's boundaries. May I never cross those lines that are for privacy's sake or that in some way would make her uncomfortable if I violated them. Help us both to establish healthy boundaries that show respect for each other. Keep us from constructing unfair or artificial boundaries that are wrongly designed to construct a private world or to cause a sense of separateness. Good boundaries enhance our marriage,

THE FEAR OF THE LORD

The fear of the LORD is the beginning of knowledge.
PROVERBS 1:7

The fear of the Lord, described in the Bible as the "beginning of knowledge," is seldom talked about these days. It's as though the fear of the Lord is no longer necessary. That wrong assumption has left many a man in deep trouble spiritually. Many marriages, too, suffer when the husband and wife don't walk in the fear of the Lord. This godly fear is sometimes described as "awe," and that's certainly part of it. But another part of it is simply refusing to do those things we know displease God. To walk in the fear of the Lord is to develop a tender conscience that is easily pricked when we violate God's standards. The fear of the Lord is a blessing in one's life, not a curse.

Lord, I honor you and fear you as the beginning of my true knowledge. This fear doesn't keep me from you; rather, it keeps me from sin. I pray you'll continue to remind me that the fear of you will always be the beginning of knowledge. It's the starting point from which all wisdom flows.

KEEPING IN STEP WITH GOD

I will instruct you and teach you
in the way you should go;
I will counsel you with my eye upon you.
PSALM 32:8

God isn't static. He moves in our lives daily. He is always on the job.

What is God doing in your life these days? How is he changing you? How is he active in your role as a husband? Are you learning more about your wife? After all, learning to be a good husband is accomplished by on-the-job training. Few men walk through marriage without being schooled in it first. Learn to listen to God as he moves in your life and marriage. Pay attention to the circumstances through which he speaks. Discover direction from his Word. Keep in step. Never. Stop. Learning.

Father in heaven, thank you for counseling me with your eye upon me. Thank you for your ongoing instruction to me as a Christian, a man, and a husband. I know I'll never master it all, but with you as my teacher, I'm making progress. Lord, may I always keep in step with what you're doing, never lagging behind. Speak, Lord, for your servant is listening.

Marriage Miracles

Nothing will be impossible with God.
Luke 1:37

God still works miracles. And that includes the miracles he performs in marriages every day. If you and your wife are happy, that itself is a miracle. How he brought you together was a miracle. And certainly in this day and age, your commitment to a lifelong marriage is a miracle in progress.

If you're presently uncertain about your marriage or if difficult times are threatening your relational happiness, then you need to ask God to bring about a miracle. Don't be hesitant; *ask and you shall receive.*

Happy or not, every marriage can be sustained by the miracle-working God.

I praise you, Lord, that you still perform miracles. You know my present need where I desire you to move miraculously in my life. I pray for a breakthrough in that situation and continued miracles in my marriage. I realize that nothing can be taken for granted. My next breath is, in a very real sense, a miracle. I pray you'll keep me believing in miracles in this age of skepticism. Your miracles keep us all alive. Praise you, Father!

THE PROMISES OF GOD

*He has granted to us his precious and very
great promises, so that through them you
may become partakers of the divine nature,
having escaped from the corruption that
is in the world because of sinful desire.*

2 PETER 1:3-4

God has given us promises in his Word designed to do two things: first, to demonstrate his faithfulness to his people. He wants us to *know* he is trustworthy. Second, he wants us to benefit from his goodness. We experience his goodness through believing his promises. God has certain promises for your marriage that you can claim and build your life together on. When you read your Bible, look for God's promises—they are for you and your wife.

God, thank you for your promises! They enable your children to become a partaker of the divine nature, escaping the corruption that's in the world because of sinful desire. With your promises, you show your faithfulness, because it's by those promises that we're able to grow spiritually. You have given promises for families, for men, and for all believers in you. Open your Word, Lord, and open my eyes to your precious and very great promises.

Grace in Marriage

The Lord be with your spirit. Grace be with you.
2 Timothy 4:22

Give grace to your partner. So she's a few minutes late. So she forgot to return your phone call right away. So she didn't congratulate you on the big deal you negotiated. You both will need grace to have a great marriage. Give it abundantly.

God, you are the Lord of grace and you extend grace to me beyond my comprehension. I pray that I might be a giver of grace to others today...and especially to my wife. Help me overlook anything I might consider a slight, realizing that I need grace from her for my slights against her—conscious and unconscious. I pray you'll make grace a centerpiece of our relationship and that we'll never fail to extend the same grace we wish to receive from the other.

HER SELF-ESTEEM

*See what kind of love the Father has given to us,
that we should be called children
of God; and so we are.*

1 JOHN 3:1

A woman's sense of self-worth comes from God. He is the primary source to affirm her value. But in human form, you are the one person who can best affirm your wife's value. Take every opportunity to remind her of how special she is. Be the human guardian of her self-worth. As you pray, ask for her to find confidence in who she is.

God, all our sense of worth comes from you. We are your handiwork. In creating my wife, you've done a masterful job. She truly is your child and a recipient of your love. Help me in my role as the human guardian and affirmer of my wife's worth. May my words of encouragement take root in her heart, establishing her more fully in your love. Use me, Lord, as a booster of my wife's sense of worth.

Sexual Surrender

Do not deprive one another, except perhaps by
agreement for a limited time, that you may
devote yourselves to prayer; but then come
together again, so that Satan may not tempt
you because of your lack of self-control.
1 Corinthians 7:5

The Bible tells us we don't own our own bodies—our spouse does. That means each partner must surrender their right to sexual intimacy. You cannot demand sex from your wife, nor can she demand it of you. Both need to sympathize with the needs of the other. Sexual compatibility is best accomplished through each partner's willingness to surrender their sexual appetites (or lack thereof) for the good of the other.

God, I thank you for my wife as the one person with whom I can share sexual intimacy. I pray that in this area we might enjoy compatibility. You know the degree to which each of us desires intimacy. Lord, we ask you to align us so that each is satisfied and neither feels deprived. May we devote ourselves to prayer in the interim when intimacy cannot be enjoyed for whatever reason. Then, O God, bring us together again as one flesh.

THE ENEMY OF MARRIAGE

Be sober-minded; be watchful. Your
adversary the devil prowls around like a
roaring lion, seeking someone to devour.
1 PETER 5:8

Though God is the friend of marriage, so too does every marriage have an enemy. Yes, even *your* marriage. We understand from Scripture that Satan is a roaring lion, seeking someone to devour—and their marriage along with it. We must not be ignorant of the enemy's tactics. We must realize the fierceness with which he attacks. Resist the devil, and he will flee. You resist; he must flee. Do not give him even a foot in the door of your marriage.

Lord, help me to be watchful and sober-minded regarding Satan's attacks on my marriage. I know the enemy seeks to devour our marriage—if not in obvious ways, then certainly little by little in subtle ways. I pray that my wife and I, not being ignorant of his devices, will resist his efforts to undermine our marriage at every turn. Remind us to walk close to you at all times. May our marriage be stronger for the resistance we employ against our enemy.

A Family's Legacy

We will not hide them from their children,
but tell to the coming generation the
glorious deeds of the LORD, and his might,
and the wonders that he has done.

PSALM 78:4

You and your wife are not a couple unto yourselves. God wants to build a legacy through you. If you and your wife have children, he wants them to be the next generation of faithful followers of Christ. That will be your family legacy. Pray to that end. Pray often for your family, and also your descendants. Who knows but that you are a man of faith due to the prayers of your ancestors?

God, I pray that my family will continue on in the faith. Give my children ears to hear and the memory to recall their legacy in future years.

Remind us to pray often for family members and for our descendants, just as some of our ancestors surely prayed for us. Create from us, O Lord, a family legacy that will honor you for generations to come.

A Beautiful Marriage

He who finds a wife finds a good thing
and obtains favor from the LORD.
PROVERBS 18:22

A beautiful marriage is ours for the asking. Oh yes, there are still things we must do to confirm our prayers. We must learn God's principles about marriage from his Word, we must then *do* them, and we must stand firm against the enemies of our marriage. But the effort is so worth it. The alternative—an ugly and unhappy marriage—is no alternative at all.

God, in my wife, you have given me a good—even great—gift. I surely have obtained favor from you. I pray for the wisdom to discern from your Word how to have a beautiful and enriching marriage. I pray for the ability to then *do* those things that make for a happy union. Then I pray for the fruit of my prayers and actions—that you will bring about the happiness my wife and I both seek.

Common Goals

Commit your way to the LORD;
trust in him, and he will act.
PSALM 37:5

A husband and wife make the best team when they share common goals. They are also less likely to drift apart. Talk often with your wife about the goals you two have settled on. Ministry? Family life? Building a business? Living off the land? Volunteerism? Whatever you do together will last—and so will your marriage.

God, I pray that my wife and I will continue to be committed to the plan you have for us. We trust in you to act on our behalf as we give you first place in our marriage. I pray that as a team of two, we can talk openly about our common goals, willing to compromise when necessary, and willing to set aside our own wishes when needed. I pray you'll continue to give us new common goals we can pursue together—with you in the midst of them.

Keeping Your Heart

Keep your heart with all vigilance,
for from it flow the springs of life.
PROVERBS 4:23

A man's heart can be a treacherous thing. It can be a traitor to his best interests, coaxing him into thoughts that lead him off the right path. A Christian man has an advantage, though. He has given his heart to the Lord and no longer has to follow the sly whispers of his lower nature. And yet some Christian men do seem to hear and follow the dictates of the fleshly heart. Thus, Scripture advises us to guard our heart. There is something within us that warrants guardianship.

God, you know my heart. It's often on fire for you and yet at other times it's drawn away by temptations or ambitions unworthy of a Christian man. Help me as I guard my heart against these distractions from righteousness. And Lord, I pray that I will keep my heart with all vigilance regarding my wife. Keep my heart only for her, desiring that she be all you've called her to be. Thank you, Father, for this heart that seeks after you.

WORTHY OF PRAISE

A woman who fears the LORD is to be praised.
PROVERBS 31:30

A good wife is worthy of her husband's high praises. Not just to her, though that's important, but also to others. Compliment your wife to other people. Make sure her reputation is known and communicate that you are blessed above all men to have her as your life's companion. She is worthy.

God, once again I return to the common prayer theme of offering thanks for the wife you've given me. She is worthy of praise as a woman of God. I thank you that she fears you and conducts herself as a godly woman. In many ways, I'm convinced I married "up." Lord, help me as I try to be the kind of husband who warrants a gift such as my wife.

MARRIAGE IS A COVENANT

*He remembers his covenant forever,
the word that he commanded, for
a thousand generations.*

PSALM 105:8

What holds a marriage together and makes it strong? The fact that it is based on a covenant before God, sealed with lifetime vows. Good men like to be known by their reputation for honesty. They like to think their word is as good as gold. What better testing ground, then, than marriage? A man who keeps his covenant with his wife, through thick and thin, is showing himself to be loyal.

Dear Lord, when I married my wife, I vowed before you and witnesses that I would be faithful to her. I renew that vow daily as I seek to be the best husband I can. You are my role model for keeping a covenant, for you have covenanted with me regarding the forgiveness of my sins, the power of your Spirit within me, and eternal life. As I look to you, I too will become a covenant keeper in all ways.

WHEN OPPOSITES ATTRACT

*The body does not consist of one
member but of many.*
1 CORINTHIANS 12:14

There's truth to the saying that opposites attract. Morning people sometimes marry night people. When she's cold, you're hot. She likes Pepsi, you like Coke. But that's really the way it should be. Marrying an opposite may be more challenging than marrying someone exactly like you, but it's a character builder. We learn compromise with someone who wants an Italian restaurant when we want Chinese. Relish the differences between you and your wife. Don't resent them.

Lord, I see in your church that you place different people in different roles. Not everyone has the same function. I get that marriage is like that too. I'm called to be a husband, not a wife. My wife is called to be a wife, not a husband. Each of us has different functions and gifts. Help me to appreciate the gifts my wife brings into our relationship, and help her to understand my gifts and my role in the family. May we learn to see our differences as something to celebrate.

HONOR HER BODY

*Do you not know that your body is a temple of
the Holy Spirit within you, whom you have
from God? You are not your own, for you were
bought with a price. So glorify God in your body.*
1 CORINTHIANS 6:19-20

A Christian's body is the temple of God. Christ lives in us. The apostle Paul tells us to honor the body. How we honor our wife's body is to treat it with respect. We don't cheapen her body or "use" it in any way. We are gentle, loving, tender, never aggressive, selfish, nor do we cause pain. Think of specific ways you can honor your wife's body.

Dear God, thank you that you have given us these wonderful human bodies in which to house the real "us." I thank you for my wife's body—her "temple of the Holy Spirit." I pray for her good health and strong energies. Help me as I honor her body by respecting it and treating it with tender care. May I never be selfish or aggressive with her body—your temple.

The Fruit of the Spirit

The fruit of the Spirit is love, joy, peace, patience, kindness, goodness, faithfulness, gentleness, self-control; against such things there is no law.
GALATIANS 5:22-23

When we walk in the Spirit, not in the flesh, we exhibit the fruit of the Spirit as the apostle Paul described. When we notice those fruit lacking, especially as we relate to our wives, we're back to walking in the flesh, with all of its ugly "fruit." That's a signal to repent and to, by faith, return to walking in the Spirit.

Father God, you have given me your Holy Spirit, who lives within me. I treasure my walk with you and I pray that the fruit of your Spirit would be manifest in my life—especially my life at home. I pray that love would dictate my actions, faithfulness would be my promise to my wife, and that self-control would be manifest in all areas of my life. Thank you for the gift of your Spirit.

Your Man Cave

*When you pray, go into your room and shut the
door and pray to your Father who is in secret.*
MATTHEW 6:6

Many husbands love to retreat to their man cave to
watch sports, read, pray in secret, or just be alone
for a while. There's nothing wrong with that—as long
as it's understood a man cave isn't where you disengage
from your family. When you're home, no matter which
room of the house you're in, you're to be readily available. A man cave may be a good occasional refuge from
worldly duties, but it's not for escaping your family.

Lord, there are times I need to be by myself. Sometimes it's to be alone with you; sometimes it's just to
relax in front of a game or take a nap. It feels good to
have that refuge. But, Father, never let it become a
refuge from my family. You've called me to be acces-
sible as a husband and father 24/7. When I'm alone,
may my heart still be with my family. Let my room
apart be a place to recharge my batteries, not an
escape hatch.

The Bible as Your Road Map

*Your word is a lamp to my feet
and a light to my path.*
Psalm 119:105

All of us husbands need good advice from time to time. The best advice we can follow is found in the Bible. Although there is great advice on how to be a husband, just as important is the advice on how to be a Christ-following man. If we do the latter, we'll do the former as well. Look to the pages of God's Word to light your way through manhood…and husbandhood.

God, without your Word to guide me, I'm clueless about how to live as a successful man or husband. As I open the Bible, I pray you'll give me the necessary insight to be the man you designed me to be. I pray that as I do what it takes to become more godly, I'll become more attentive and diligent as well. Open my eyes, Father, as I take your Word as the lamp for my feet and the light for my path.

Servant Leadership

Let the greatest among you become as the youngest,
and the leader as one who serves.
LUKE 22:26

The term *servant leadership* sounds like an oxymoron. One either serves or one leads…right? Perhaps so in secular terms, but as Christians we understand that leading *is* serving when done biblically. If we serve as a boost to our ego, we're not truly serving according to God's definition. The true motive of servant leadership is love. If we love our wives, we will serve them through gentle leadership. We see servant leadership modeled for us in Christ himself. He led us into new life through the ultimate act of service—sacrificing his life for our sin.

It's a high calling to serve our wives by leading. Let's do it right.

God, I often see leaders in the world lording it over those they lead. I know that's not your way of serving. In your kingdom, it's upside down: We lead by serving others. Let it be my goal to become the kind of husband my wife is anxious to follow because she sees my motivation is love. Lord, may I lead by following Jesus's sacrificial example.

HEART LOYALTY

I say to you that everyone who looks at a
woman with lustful intent has already
committed adultery with her in his heart.
MATTHEW 5:28

Wives prize a loyal husband. She wants to know you're true blue to her. That you'll stand by her, no matter what. She'll know how loyal you are by how loyal you are first in little things. Your very attitude can project loyalty. Loyalty isn't just for Boy Scouts—it's for husbands too.

God, you know how my eyes can wander, even when I don't want them to. I pray you'll help me safeguard against adultery in my heart. As I determine to put only pure images in my mind, I pray that the effect will be pure images appearing on the movie screen of my mind throughout the day. Help me be loyal to my wife not just in body, but also in mind. There is no one but her, Lord.

THESE FEW SHORT YEARS

What is your life? For you are a mist that
appears for a little time and then vanishes.
JAMES 4:14

The older you get, the faster time flies. Your lifespan may be seventy years…or more, if God so wills. But even seven decades is short when you think about it. We seem to have more opportunities and possibilities than we have years. We must be good stewards of the years God gives us. Your marriage, too, is brief compared to eternity. Treasure each day as though it's the last. Make the most of the gift of time.

God, I believe you have the day of my departure from this earth already determined. Until then, you've given me much to enjoy in the few short years of a lifetime. I take none of it for granted. I want to be a good steward of the treasures you've given me—and a good steward of my time and the opportunities you send my way. Thank you for my marriage and the years my wife and I share. May those years multiply both in time and happiness. Thank you, Lord, for each precious hour you give me.

COOLING OFF

Whoever is slow to anger is better than the mighty,
and he who rules his spirit than he who takes a city.
PROVERBS 16:32

What husband hasn't said something in the heat of the moment that he wishes he could take back? We've all been there. Through our experience we should grasp the realization that every disagreement should come with an intermission that permits a time-out or cooling-off period, during which time we collect our thoughts, eat our words, and commit to reacting reasonably instead of through anger. Stay cool, husband. Stay cool.

God, sometimes I have a big mouth. I speak when I should remain silent and cool off after something has ticked me off. Help me keep my temper as I teach myself to become slow to anger. Help me rule my spirit and be stronger than a commander who takes a city. Most of all, help me not to offend my wife by spouting off in a disagreement with words I'll later regret. Keep me cool, Lord.

Seasons of a Marriage

For everything there is a season, and a
time for every matter under heaven.
Ecclesiastes 3:1

A marriage, like life itself, passes through several seasons. Early on we're young, passionate, and eager for all that lies ahead. As time passes, we become focused on additional things—our career, kids, responsibilities, perhaps ministry. Later, our passions might not burn so hot, but more as glowing embers. Companionship becomes as important to us as intimacy once was. Oh, the intimacy is still there, but it, like the rest of life, has mellowed into something fine.

A wise couple will anticipate the seasons of their marriage and thank God for them. He means for every season to be beautiful. Whichever one you're in now, enjoy it.

Lord, as our marriage passes through its seasons, give us quality time apart. Allow us space to breathe between laps in what seems to be the rat race of this season of life. Thank you for every season we pass through. Remind us always to enjoy the present season because someday we will look back and wish we had been more appreciative for the good times of this season.

Wisdom

Who is wise and understanding among you?
By his good conduct let him show his
works in the meekness of wisdom.

JAMES 3:13

Wisdom cannot be purchased. It sometimes can't even be taught. In fact, someone has defined wisdom as knowledge applied correctly. The best wisdom comes from God, not from books written by men or women. And wisdom is most definitely indispensable for a happy marriage. Husbands must prayerfully and carefully develop wisdom as they lead their family. Watch for God to set up unique life experiences through which you can learn how to apply wisdom.

Lord, I need your wisdom to lead my family. I need something beyond human resources. I pray for the kind of divine wisdom that leads to good conduct and an effective life as a husband. I pray for my wife today, that she would know that I lean on you for wisdom and not on my own understanding as I guide our family.

The Danger of Comparison

Not that we dare to classify or compare ourselves
with some of those who are commending
themselves. But when they measure themselves
by one another and compare themselves with
one another, they are without understanding.

2 Corinthians 10:12

Comparing ourselves with others is dangerous. God's work in us is unique. Comparison only invites envy. As for marriage, one of the worst things a husband can do is compare his wife unfavorably with another wife, a previous girlfriend, or even his mother. (Never compare your wife's cooking or housekeeping unfavorably with your mother's!) Love the wife you have. She's meant for you. No one else will do.

Lord, keep me from the foolishness of comparing myself with others. Let me not become envious or covetous of others. Give to me only what is good or instructive for me. Help me to be content with your will, be it simple or vast. Thank you for my wife. I will not compare her to anyone else. I'm content in knowing you have assigned me the task of being a good husband. Neither, then, do I compare myself with other husbands.

THE UNPLUGGED MARRIAGE

Be still before the LORD and wait patiently for him.
PSALM 37:7

Sometimes we as couples need to unplug ourselves from our techno-world and spend time together. Forget Facebook and do real face time with each other over a romantic dinner. Turn off the TV and reminisce with your loved one. Silence your cell phone. Remember, marriage is a relationship, not another app.

Dear Lord, technology is great, but it can become an obsession. Help me monitor my time on devices that take me into cyberspace, away from reality. Keep me from the habit of pulling up a game when I should be communicating with my wife or the kids. Help me instill that same discipline in the rest of the family. Teach us to have unplugged fun and conversation instead of texting or putting buds in our ears.

Saying Good-Bye
to Addiction

Wine is a mocker, strong drink a brawler,
and whoever is led astray by it is not wise.
Proverbs 20:1

Addiction is a killer. Literally. It kills people and ends marriages. The abuse of drugs, alcohol, or sex can start slow. One doesn't become a slave to their substance of choice overnight. Likewise, ending your addiction may take time. It may take counseling or an accountability partner. *Do whatever it takes.* Don't let pride or fear of shame hold you back.

If you have no addictions, you may know someone who is addicted. Pray for an end to the bondage.

God, addiction is taking a terrible toll on families. Mostly men, it seems, are addicted and in the wake of their bondage they leave much destruction. Destroyed families, fatherless children, brokenhearted parents. Lord, I pray for those I know who are bound to an addictive substance. I pray for ministries and recovery groups helping those in bondage. To the extent that I'm tempted to addiction, I pray for my own spiritual health. Keep me strong, Lord. And show me how to help others.

Variety, the Spice of Life

*Delight yourself in the LORD, and he will
give you the desires of your heart.*
PSALM 37:4

Marriages grow stale because every night turns into the same as last night. We get into a routine and grind away until something jolts us into change. Don't wait for that when it comes to your marriage. Spice it up. Do something you've never done before. Take a weekend away to someplace you've never been. Volunteer together at a crisis pregnancy center or some other ministry; take in a musical venue that's new to you both. Make efforts to keep your marriage fresh.

God, thank you for the variety of ways I can show my love for my wife. I pray for more creative ways for us to celebrate our love. Help me as I try to steer us away from a routine life. Give us common interests we can pursue together. Open doors we may not be anticipating. Help us keep our love fresh, Lord.

LEGALISM IS A KILLER

Do not let what you regard as good be spoken of
as evil. For the kingdom of God is not a matter
of eating and drinking but of righteousness
and peace and joy in the Holy Spirit.
ROMANS 14:16-17

Pity the poor wife whose husband holds her to a list of demands. Legalism—the withholding of approval based on one's performance of required duties—kills us spiritually and smothers marriages. Give your wife freedom; give her grace. Never withhold your affection for not complying with your desires. And keep in mind legalism can be subtle. If you're unsure whether you've been holding her (or each other) to an unreasonable standard of behavior, then ask your wife for her input.

Dear God, legalism is such a killer. Grace, when understood properly—and not as license—frees us to serve you through love. Guide me as I lead our household through grace, not through legalism. May my wife and family know that my love for them does not waver—it is not based on the performance of certain duties, but unconditional. May I realize that, too, about your love for me.

Giving Up the Good
for the Best

By this we know love, that he
laid down his life for us,
and we ought to lay down our lives for the brothers.
1 John 3:16

When we were single, we did pretty much what we pleased. But as married men, we have new considerations. Now we must forgo some pleasures from the past—hanging out with the guys, a time-consuming hobby, or taking off for a weekend of skiing. Good things, to be sure. But sometimes the good is the enemy of the best. And for a married man, the best is time with his wife. Hobbies and pastimes remain important, but a good husband will learn how to prioritize his interests—after his wife.

Lord, you've brought a lot of good things into my life over the years, some of which I still enjoy. Sometimes I may not sense when it's time to let some things go. Please show me when I'm putting something good ahead of what's best for me. If my wife is the source of this revelation, so be it. Help me as I lay down my life—even the good in my life—for my wife.

Loving by Faith

We walk by faith, not by sight.
2 Corinthians 5:7

When love as a romantic feeling isn't there, does that mean love is dead? No, not at all. Feelings in marriage come and go. When they "go," we still have the opportunity to love our wife by faith. We know loving our spouse is God's will, so we can pray for our spouse and love her by faith, not by feelings. The funny thing is when we love by faith, the feelings generally return. And don't forget, sometimes your wife has to love *you* by faith too.

God, you know I do love my wife. Sometimes, though, the feelings of love come and go. When I don't really feel love, I feel like something must be wrong with me. Yet I know I *do* love her. At such times, Lord, I will love her by faith and trust the romantic feelings will return. After all, I know I love you, yet sometimes I feel very unspiritual. I love you by faith and I love my wife by faith, knowing there are times when she loves me by faith as well.

A Pure Thought Life

In all circumstances take up the shield
of faith, with which you can extinguish
all the flaming darts of the evil one.
EPHESIANS 6:16

Sometimes the thoughts come at us faster than we can deal with them. You know the thoughts I refer to. The temptations to lust, hate, be angry, worry, doubt—all these and more are like darts thrown into our mind by our mortal enemy. And, sure enough, that's just what they are: Satan's darts designed to take us down through an impure thought life. What does Paul recommend? When the darts are flying at you, put up the shield of faith. Reject those thoughts. And replace them with positive, praiseworthy thoughts.

Lord, I often return to praying about my thought life. May I renew my mind through your Word and reject evil thoughts as fast as they come by holding up the shield of faith against the flaming darts of the evil one. Father, help me turn my mind to the good, pure, honorable things when I am tempted by impurity, doubt, or fear. As I turn my mind to you and your attributes, I'm able to conquer wayward thoughts.

Ordinary Husbands

The LORD will fulfill his purpose for me.
PSALM 138:8

Sometimes our imaginations, often fed by the media, hold out a sort of phantom perfect husband. He never forgets to kiss his wife, he's handy around the house, he has the perfect job, and he brings home a nice paycheck. He looks like Ryan Gosling or George Clooney. When we compare ourselves with this phantom perfect husband, we come up short. *Way* short. But, in fact, there are no perfect husbands. There are only ordinary husbands learning to be better men as they rely on God. Don't compare yourself. God isn't comparing you to anyone.

God, I'm such an ordinary guy. I'm not all that special in the world's eyes. I often fall short at home. My wife knows that better than anyone. But Lord, you use ordinary people every day. What's more, Christ died for someone as ordinary as me. You place the value of this ordinary man as the value of your beloved son, whom you gave so that I can enjoy fellowship with you. That's the amazing thing—that *you* would desire fellowship with ordinary people. For that, Lord, I bow down and offer praise.

Honoring God on the Job

*Whatever you do, in word or deed, do
everything in the name of the Lord Jesus,
giving thanks to God the Father through him.*
Colossians 3:17

A Christian man doesn't only strive to be a better husband; he also wants to excel at his job. In addition to providing him with income, a job gives him a way to "do everything in the name of the Lord Jesus." A strong work ethic is a great witness for the Lord and a way to honor him. Satisfaction with one's work is a joy for any man. If your work situation leaves you frustrated, it likely shows up at home. It does no harm for you to reevaluate, every year or so, whether this is where God wants you to stay. Frustration and a lack of joy may mean it's time to move on.

God, on my job, may others see in me a work ethic that reflects my faith. When it's time to move on, I pray you'll make it clear. Wherever I work, I pray you'll allow me to be productive. And remind me to leave my frustrations at work and not bring them home to my wife.

SELF-CONTROL

*A man without self-control is like a city
broken into and left without walls.*
PROVERBS 25:28

The fruit of the Spirit is...self-control.
GALATIANS 5:22-23

One evidence of a man yielded to the Spirit is self-control. If a man doesn't have control of himself through the power of the Holy Spirit, who *is* in control of his life? A wife respects a husband who practices restraint when it comes to his moods, passions, anger, strength, and words—all of which, when out of control, can damage a marriage. By faith, every husband can walk in the Spirit and keep himself under control.

Lord, thank you for the Holy Spirit within me, who helps me gain control of myself—my words, actions, attitudes are all submitted to your Spirit to be used in positive ways. I understand how it is to lose control of one's self—to be like a city with broken-down walls where invaders and enemies can easily enter in. God, guide me through your Spirit. Let me be a self-controlled husband at home, not given to fluctuating emotions. Help me to stay calm and collected.

INVESTING IN MARRIAGE

Lay up for yourselves treasures in heaven,
where neither moth nor rust destroys and
where thieves do not break in and steal.
MATTHEW 6:20

Our best investment as men is in our families. It's there that we deposit our gifts and our faith in God to bring about a good return on our investment. Never hesitate to deposit more in your marriage account. The dividends are terrific!

God, every investment a good man makes is expected to yield a return—a profit. I pray that what I invest in my role as a husband will be richly profitable for me, my wife, and my family. It's easy for even a wise investor to make a risky or poor investment at times—with the accompanying loss. Lord, keep my eyes open as I invest in being a good husband. Keep me from those poor investments that will not only be unprofitable, but may also erode the initial investment. Help me as I trust you to bring a good return on this precious investment of being a husband.

THE HUSBAND WHO READS

*When you come, bring the cloak that I left
with Carpus at Troas, also the books,
and above all the parchments.*
PAUL TO TIMOTHY IN 2 TIMOTHY 4:13

Most men find themselves crunched for time, leaving few hours for simple pleasures like reading. How does reading benefit a man—especially in his role as a husband? The Bible is, of course, full of great advice on how to live as a godly man. But other books can be helpful too. Whether your tastes favor John Eldredge's *Wild at Heart* or theology from John Piper—or fast-moving fiction from Ted Dekker or Frank Peretti—just be careful of what you read. Remember the old adage: garbage in, garbage out.

God, thank you for your Word. When I read it, I come away with a blessing. Thank you for the gift of reading. Thank you for giving others the gift of writing books and articles that can entertain me, help me grow as a believer, and make me a better husband. I pray for more time to read—and for access to the right kind of reading. Speak to me, Lord, through the written word.

Fear Not

*Fear not, for I am with you; be not dismayed, for I
am your God; I will strengthen you, I will help you,
I will uphold you with my righteous right hand.*
ISAIAH 41:10

Every man has his fears. Even Indiana Jones feared snakes. Some men fear a poor economy affecting their portfolio. Others fear cancer. Some fear what the future holds. And some husbands fear their role as leader of the family. But no matter what our fear, God commands us to "fear not." There is no fear that the love of God cannot conquer. Don't be intimidated by your fears. Overcome them in the power of the Lord.

God, you know my fears. You know what causes me to doubt and worry. Yet I know you are sovereign. Nothing can happen that doesn't go through you first—which is why I can entrust all to you.

Sometimes, Lord, I fear my role as leader of my family. I don't want to fail in this. Give me wisdom. Show me how to lead as you do—gently, but with purpose. Mold me as a leader, God. Mold me as a man.

HEALING THE HURTS
IN MARRIAGE

*There is one whose rash words are like sword
thrusts, but the tongue of the wise brings healing.*
PROVERBS 12:18

You said or did something…or she said or did something, and now someone is in pain. You're not alone. Every married person experiences pain at times from their spouse. It's how you handle the pain that determines what will happen next. Will you apologize, even if you feel you're right? It's a no-brainer that if you love your wife, you don't want to see her hurt. The things that heal hurts in marriage are praying together, apologies, a sense of humor, laying down one's "rights," and finally, time.

Lord, I don't think I realized that when I got married there would be times when I would hurt the one I love or that she would hurt me. But then it happened. One of us said words to the other that were like sword thrusts—and pain resulted. God, when that happens again, help each of us to rush to offer the first apology. Let us resolve to have tongues that bring healing, not pain.

A Wife's Wiring

A fool takes no pleasure in understanding,
but only in expressing his opinion.
PROVERBS 18:2

To no one's surprise, women are wired differently than men. You'll find marriage a lifelong graduate course in understanding your wife's uniqueness and the appropriate responses to her emotional and physical needs. Pay attention to her needs, not all of which she will tell you.

God, we men are wired so differently from our wives. I sometimes wonder why she doesn't "get it" when I try to express a profound opinion. And there are times when I don't follow her reasoning. She's just wired so... *feminine*. Help me, Lord, to accept that her wiring is your design for her, just as you wired me the way I am. Thank you that—wiring differences and all—she's the right woman for me.

IDENTIFYING THE STRESSES ON YOUR MARRIAGE

Do not be anxious about anything,
but in everything by prayer and
supplication with thanksgiving let your
requests be made known to God.
PHILIPPIANS 4:6

There are benefits to praying about the things that bring stress to your marriage. First, it helps you to identify what's causing the stress. That may include your finances, in-law issues, children, keeping up the household, sexual compatibility, overwork, fatigue, unrealistic expectations. No matter what the cause, pray for guidance on how to handle the matter. Then follow God's lead and do what you must to eliminate the stress.

God, sometimes prayer is more of an afterthought when it comes to the things that cause stress in our marriage. Yet prayer should always be our first course of action. You know what sets us off. You know what we need to do to remove or lessen our stress triggers. Lord, help me to overcome the anxiety caused by stress by resting in you with a heart of thanks, May I always remember to make my requests known to you.

YOUR WIFE'S PRAYERS

If you abide in me, and my words abide in you,
ask whatever you wish, and it will be done for you.
JOHN 15:7

As you pray for your wife daily, make sure you ask her to pray for you too. You need her prayers. She knows you better than anyone else on earth, and she sees your needs daily. As for the needs she doesn't see, you need to let her know about them. When a new need arises, share it with her. Keep your best prayer partner informed.

God, thank you for my prayer-partner wife. I pray for her needs today, and I pray you'll give her a fresh wind of your Spirit in her life. Go before her today and protect her from danger. Help her overcome her doubts and fears. And Lord, please remind her to pray for me. Help me be more open with her about my needs. You will surely answer her prayers on my behalf.

A United Front

*Finally, all of you, have unity of
mind, sympathy, brotherly love,
a tender heart, and a humble mind.*
1 PETER 3:8

You and your wife are one. You're a united front
against all comers. If you have children, you know
how they can pit one parent against the other. "Well,
Dad said…" "Well, Mom said…" and so it goes. No
matter the source of the trouble, you two need to stand
together.

Lord God, thank you for giving me such a stalwart
companion as we stand together against adversity
and, at the same time, share the joys you've provided
for us. May all we do together be done as a united two-
some, able to stand against all comers. I pray for our
continued unity, and that we'll have tender hearts and
humble minds as we stand strong together.

YOUR WIFE COMES FIRST

Let each one of you love his wife as himself.
EPHESIANS 5:33

We husbands have many interests—our job, our hobbies, following sports, hanging with the guys. So many activities compete for our time with the result that our families—and particularly our wives—are bumped into second or third place…or even lower. Even husbands who are in the ministry must be careful that their church duties don't usurp the place the wife holds. If you're a husband, your wife comes first. And she needs to know it.

Father, I'm a busy man. I thank you for all the activities in my life. But help me to recognize when I need to cut back so I don't shortchange my wife and family. Remind me that my wife comes first; may I view pleasing her as being the same as if I were pleasing myself. Give me the ability to rightly order my life's activities and let go of those that derail me from higher priorities.

"Don't Go There"

*One thing I do: forgetting what lies behind
and straining forward to what lies ahead, I
press on toward the goal for the prize of
the upward call of God in Christ Jesus.*
Philippians 3:13-14

Every couple needs to know their "Don't Go There" topics. These are areas of potential conflict that must be avoided. The *d* word (divorce) is one such topic. No bringing outsiders (except qualified counselors) into your disagreements. No running home to Mama's house. No disrespectful talk. Consider certain topics best left unsaid in your house. A past romance? A regrettable financial decision? An auto accident?

God, I know a few of our "Don't Go There" topics. Divorce is one. And there are other things we need to be mindful of. Sometimes when something goes wrong, it seems like one or both of us play the blame game. May we not go there. Give us wisdom to avoid talking about things that lead to spats and accomplish nothing. Help us as we extend grace to the other in place of blame. Teach us to steer clear of unwholesome talk. Guide us as we press on for the prize.

Passing the Faith On

*These words that I command you today shall be
on your heart. You shall teach them diligently
to your children, and shall talk of them when
you sit in your house, and when you walk by the
way, and when you lie down, and when you rise.*
DEUTERONOMY 6:6-7

As the saying goes, God has no grandchildren. Every person must come to the place of choosing to follow or deny Christ. You and your wife have the responsibility of making Christ as Lord a desirable decision for your children. Your faith (or lack thereof) will largely affect what they come to believe. Live as a couple in such a way as to pass the faith on easily and at an early age.

God, I praise you for the examples of faith you've allowed me to know. Now, Lord, I know others—especially my children—watch me as an example of faith, and I pray I can be a positive witness to them. Help me as I speak of you to my children. I pray that in me, their father, they catch a glimpse of you, their heavenly Father.

THE LONELY MARRIAGE

*In the same way husbands should love
their wives as their own bodies.
He who loves his wife loves himself.*
EPHESIANS 5:28

When God instituted marriage, it was so man would not be alone. Eve was company for Adam, just as he was company for her. Not all marriages share a deep companionship, though. Some marriages are more on paper than of the heart. These lonely marriages miss God's best for the couple. The thing is, lonely marriages don't usually happen overnight. They build slowly, over time. Consider your marriage. Are you and your wife true companions—or are you drifting apart? If so, don't let that continue. Don't let a lonely marriage (for *either* of you) rob you both of God's blessing in marriage.

God, you created marriage so that man and woman wouldn't be alone in life. Yet sometimes even in my marriage I can feel alone. I'm sure my wife feels the same way. Lord, these feelings are not your will for us. Help us both realize we were created to be there for the other. Increase our affections for each other. Lord, renew our love.

CLEANING UP OUR MESSES

*Arise, for it is your task, and we are
with you; be strong and do it.*
EZRA 10:4

Some husbands are notorious for not cleaning up after themselves. Dirty clothes miss the laundry basket, the toilet seat is left up, dishes aren't taken to the kitchen. We can do better. We can pick up after ourselves and not expect our wives to act as our personal janitor. Be considerate. What can you do with the mess you've made that will save your wife time (and resentment)?

Father God, help me as I strive to be orderly and well-disciplined. Remind me—when I'm leaving something behind that is my responsibility—to clean things up or put them away. Thank you for a kind wife who has often done tasks that should have fallen to me. Help me "be strong and do it" when it comes to the tasks that are mine.

Denying Yourself

If anyone would come after me,
let him deny himself and take up
his cross daily and follow him.
Luke 9:23

The essence of our faith is to deny ourselves and follow Christ. We're not our own; we belong to him. Similarly, we, as married men, are no longer our own. We belong to another and must deny ourselves to please our wives. In an ideal marriage, the wife denies herself for her husband as well. But not all marriages are ideal. You're not responsible for your wife's self-denial—only your own.

God, self-denial is painful. My human tendency is to want to affirm myself, not deny myself. But now that I'm a married man, I know I'm no longer my own. Not only do I belong to you as a Christian, but I also belong to my wife as her husband. Though painful, I pray for a greater experience at self-denial. As I look at Jesus's example, I hear his call for his followers to do likewise. By your Spirit, Lord, I know I can do all things...even deny myself.

"I Appreciate All You Do"

We give thanks to God always for all of you,
constantly mentioning you in our prayers.
1 Thessalonians 1:2

A few simple words can mean a lot to our wives. They want our love, protection, attention. And they want us to appreciate what they do for us. Every day we need to find a way to tell our wife how much we appreciate her. Sometimes it will be with those simple words. Other days we may find a tangible way to *show* our appreciation, to demonstrate that we don't take her love for granted.

Lord, when I forget to show my appreciation to my wife, jog my memory. As I look around the house or eat a delicious dinner or put on a clean shirt, remind me to be thankful. Remind me to say the words of appreciation my wife needs to hear and that I really do mean—and not just for what she does. I want her to know I appreciate her for who she is and for taking on the dubious task of loving me.

ALWAYS A BRIDE

*I saw the holy city, new Jerusalem, coming
down out of heaven from God,
prepared as a bride adorned for her husband.*
REVELATION 21:2

Time ages us all. You're not the same groom you were of yesteryear. Your wife may no longer resemble the bride she was on your wedding day. Yet true love is ageless. Husbands do well to always think of their wife as their bride, no matter her age. It's a reminder of how much you still love the woman who pledged her troth to you.

Lord, my bride is beautiful in my eyes. Now and forever. Thank you for both her outer and inner beauty. Keep me in remembrance of how radiant she was on our wedding day. May the joy we both felt then continue on for many years. When our routine and adverse circumstances try to rob us of that joy, please remind us of the everlasting joy we have in you.

WIPING HER TEARS

He will wipe away every tear from their eyes,
and death shall be no more, neither shall there
be mourning, nor crying, nor pain anymore,
for the former things have passed away.
REVELATION 21:4

Among many other things, you are your wife's comforter. During your years together, she will shed many tears. Your role will often be to hold her hand, listen to her, and wipe away her tears. Most often your presence will simply be enough. Be there.

Lord, my wife isn't often sad. I don't see many tears from her. But when I do, may I be there for her. I know one of my husbandly roles is to be her comforter, to wipe away her tears, to hold her tight in times of sadness. God, give me the sensitivity to be what she needs during such down times. Help me provide the strong shoulders she needs to lean on. Help me be fully there when she needs my comfort.

That Ring on Your Finger

On that day, declares the LORD of hosts, I will
take you, O Zerubbabel my servant, the son
of Shealtiel, declares the LORD, and make you
like a signet ring, for I have chosen you.
HAGGAI 2:23

That wedding band on the third finger of your left hand is there as a sign of your never-ending love and commitment to your wife. Whenever you glance at it, take time to think about its significance. Then, once again, thank God for bringing her to you.

God, in your Word it's recorded that you took Zerubbabel as your servant and fashioned a ring as a token of having chosen him. Lord, I have a ring from my wife to indicate she has chosen me to be her one and only for a lifetime. I pray I will always look at that ring and consider the significance of it. She has chosen *me*. What a wondrous thing! Thank you for this great miracle, Lord.

CHANGE

*Jesus Christ is the same yesterday
and today and forever.*
HEBREWS 13:8

There's a saying that women marry men hoping they'll change, but they never do. Men marry women hoping they'll never change, and they always do. That saying brings a smile, but the truth is that both husband and wife *do* change in the course of a lifetime. We all do. Expecting change and accepting the modifications that come with it is crucial. Don't be rattled at the changes as they come. Accept them and adapt.

Father, I know change is part of life. We all change... including me. I pray that as I age and go through changes, they would be good ones that benefit my wife. I pray for her as well. Lord, walk us slowly through the times ahead as we face changes we're not even aware of right now. And thank you, Father, that you never change. We can rely on your steadfastness at all times. Keep our love alive as we change.

HER OPINION MATTERS

She opens her mouth with wisdom, and the
teaching of kindness is on her tongue.
PROVERBS 31:26

Wives seem to be gifted with insight many husbands lack. Too often we go off on our own making some seemingly wise decision, which, had we talked to our wives, we may have decided differently. Value your wife's words. God has given her gifts you can't do without.

God, thank you that in marriage it's like having twice the wisdom—maybe even more. I hear great and wise words from my wife, and there is surely kindness on her tongue. I value her greatly and listen diligently when she speaks. Lord, please continue to speak to me through my wife. May she, in turn, come to value my opinion as well. Give us listening ears, Lord, to hear wisdom from each other.

Staying Healthy
for Your Wife

Beloved, I pray that all may go well with
you and that you may be in good health,
as it goes well with your soul.
3 John 2

A healthy marriage is wonderful. So is a healthy husband. If you would enjoy a long life with your wife, take care of yourself. Eat right, exercise, and develop your spiritual life. When your health breaks down, you aren't the only one who suffers—the entire family is affected. Do right by your wife and children by doing right by your body.

God, I need your help when it comes to staying healthy. As I age, my metabolism is slowing down. I don't always eat right when I'm in a hurry. My exercise plan is sometimes hit or miss. But despite this, I do want to live out a full life, just as you have planned for me. Help me, I pray, set my health in order. Help me to decrease my stress, choose the right foods, exercise more, and keep a positive attitude. Renew my energies, Lord. Renew my youthfulness.

Lean in to Love

Love bears all things, believes all things,
hopes all things, endures all things.
Love never ends.
1 Corinthians 13:7-8

If you're like most husbands, you have a lot on your plate: work, finances, chores around the house, kids... and so on. But there must always be time to lean in to love. That is, to realize you've been taking much for granted, not continuing the pursuit of your wife as your lover. Wives want that. They need to be reassured of your love, and often. Lean in to your wife and lean in to love.

Father, I'm thankful for your description of love as bearing, believing, hoping, and enduring all things. That's the kind of love I want my wife to experience from me. Though I'm often busy, I must not become too busy to lean in and lavish my love on my wife. True love—your kind of love—never ends. May that be true of my love for my wife too.

THE FINE ART OF CUDDLING

His left hand is under my head,
and his right hand embraces me!
SONG OF SOLOMON 8:3

I s your wife a cuddler? If so, you're blessed. Cuddling is a great stress reliever, a great way to keep warm on a winter's night, and a physical way of showing affection. Take the initiative and cuddle often. Soon you'll be an expert.

God, I know my wife loves to be near me physically. She rejoices at my touch. We enjoy being together on the couch or in bed cuddling close to each other. That physical closeness enhances our emotional love for each other. Lord, let me always be available when cuddling is the need of the day.

Initiate Romance

My dove, my perfect one, is the only one,
the only one of her mother,
pure to her who bore her.
Song of Solomon 6:9

Wives like it when the husband is the initiator in romance. They like to be pursued (and caught!). Of course, you'll always want to be sensitive to timing. Sometimes it's not practical. It could be she's just not in the mood or she's busy or too tired. When that's the case, back off. Just know that initiating romance is appreciated by most wives.

God, you initiated my relationship with you by pursuing me...and you caught me. I praise you for your love that seeks out your beloved. Now as a husband, I understand the joy of being pursued by one who loves you and I give that pleasure to my wife as I pursue her and initiate romance. Lord, help me to be responsive to signals that this isn't a good time for romance and back off. When the time is right, help me to lovingly pursue her with tenderness.

Giving Money Away

Every man shall give as he is able,
according to the blessing
of the Lord your God that he has given you.
Deuteronomy 16:17

As you and your wife decide which ministries to support financially, it's wise to remember that money given to the furtherance of God's kingdom or to help people is a wise investment. Generous givers seldom have money problems. Never donate grudgingly. Be a cheerful and generous giver, along with your prayer support.

God, you have been generous with us. Though we have needs, we don't let that stop us from giving to others, including ministries you've laid on our hearts. I pray that my wife and I would be open to more giving as you bless us financially. Bring to our attention the needs in our own church fellowship as well as at other ministries so we can share what we have, just as the people in the early church did. Lord, multiply our giving by multiplying our ability to give.

The Joy of the Lord

The joy of the LORD is your strength.
NEHEMIAH 8:10

The Christian life is a joyful life. We are blessed to have the joy of the Lord as one of the fruit of the Spirit. Exhibiting joy in our roles as husbands is crucial. A joyless marriage is drudgery. Consider that the joy of the Lord is your strength, not only personally, but also in your marriage.

Father, you have given me great joy in Christ. I am a blessed man and I rejoice in all that you've given me, especially my wife. I pray for our mutual joy, that it might be centered in you and that it might increase with time. Help us keep joy alive in our home, even amid adversity when it comes. Praise you, God, that you have so designed it that your joy is actually our source of strength. When we would be strong, we must rejoice.

Marriage Memories

I thank my God in all my remembrance of you,
always in every prayer of mine for you all making
my prayer with joy, because of your partnership
in the gospel from the first day until now.
PHILIPPIANS 1:3-5

One of God's greatest gifts to mankind is that of memories. A good marriage is, in itself, a long-term opportunity to build a treasure trove of memories. In this day of cell phone photography, don't forget to print and transfer some of your memory-making photos to a traditional album that can be reviewed now and then. Enlarge the best photos and place a couple of them on your office wall or in your living room.

Always be on the lookout for opportunities to make new memories with your wife.

Lord, as I look back on my life, I can remember some wonderful memories of times my wife and I have enjoyed. I treasure these moments as gifts from you. I pray that someday we'll look back on our present situation with fondness. Grant us, Lord, the opportunity to become even richer in stored memories. And may we recall your presence in every glorious memory.

IN ALL THINGS, GIVE THANKS

*Give thanks in all circumstances; for this is
the will of God in Christ Jesus for you.*
1 THESSALONIANS 5:18

Giving thanks when things are going well is easy. But God commands us to give thanks in *all* things. Are you stressed? Give thanks anyway. Are you in financial trouble? Give thanks anyway. Is your home life under attack? Give thanks. By doing so, you're saying to God you're not going to allow this rough patch to get you down or cause you to doubt. Instead, you're going to thank God in this situation because you acknowledge that he is still in control and can bring about a right resolution. Yes, in *all* things.

Lord, "all things" eventually happen in every marriage, including mine. I know I can give thanks no matter what circumstances my wife and I find ourselves in. In every case, good or bad, we can give thanks. Father, even today with our present situation, we give thanks. You are Lord and nothing is impossible for you. Be our strength for today.

LEADING IS NOT DOMINATING

*I want you to understand that the head of
every man is Christ, the head of a wife is her
husband, and the head of Christ is God.*
1 CORINTHIANS 11:3

Down through the ages, many husbands have browbeaten their wives over leadership and submission. The husband leads and the wife goes along with whatever the husband dictates, right? But love doesn't work that way. Leadership is serving, not dominating. Many men may want to call the shots in the marriage, but how many want to serve by laying down their lives for the woman they love? Lead, don't dominate.

God, as I figure out this leadership role I have, I pray you'll help my wife be patient with me. Teach me as I go, Lord, mistakes and all. Help me as I put on the attitude of serving my family, of being a giver...just as you are. Lord, keep me from dominating my wife; rather, may I complement her.

No Private Worlds

We have renounced disgraceful, underhanded ways.
2 Corinthians 4:2

The opposite of transparency is for husbands (or wives) to have private worlds into which the spouse may not enter or even be aware of. For a happily married couple, neither spouse should have such a private world, nor harbor any secret "second" lives. Being transparent and having nothing hidden, private, or secret from your spouse is a key to a successful marriage.

God, sometimes it's tempting to want to escape into a private world or even have a second life that's truly mine. But that, Lord, is selfishness on my part. I renounce such disgraceful, underhanded ideas. What my wife sees is what she gets. No secret fantasy worlds, no hidden life. The open life you've provided is a blessing for me...and it is enough.

A Secure Future

I have set the LORD always before me; because
he is at my right hand, I shall not be shaken.
PSALM 16:8

It's understandable to be concerned about the future. We live in dangerous times when almost anything, even the unthinkable, can happen. For a Christian, though, God has not changed with these dangerous times. He's still the Lord of our lives, isn't he? What, then, about the future can we possibly fear? With him, our future is secure. Carry that sense of security into your marriage and family life. Never allow fear of the future to be the dominant emotion in your family life.

God, for my future, I trust in you. I fear nothing that may come my way. I'm not afraid of financial difficulty, disease, job loss, or natural disasters because I know you're sovereign and will not let anything come my way that I can't handle. I will not be shaken in my faith because I have set you before me. I am strong in you.

STRENGTHEN YOURSELF IN THE LORD YOUR GOD

*David was greatly distressed, for the people spoke
of stoning him, because all the people were bitter
in soul, each for his sons and daughters. But
David strengthened himself in the LORD his God.*

1 SAMUEL 30:6

David was having a hard time of it. In fact, he was "greatly distressed." People were so bitter they were ready to stone him. So what did David do? Under great stress, he "strengthened himself in the LORD his God." From time to time, we all need to do that—even on days when we're not threatened with stoning.

Father, I've never had it as bad as David, but I've sure had my share of hard days. Some at work, some at home. Lord, when that happens, I need to turn immediately to you. I need to strengthen myself in you. Maybe you even allow difficulties for that very reason. Help me make the most use of my distressing days, Father, and welcome me as I come to you for fresh strength.

FORGIVE YOURSELF

If we confess our sins, he is faithful
and just to forgive us our sins
and to cleanse us from all unrighteousness.
1 JOHN 1:9

We husbands aren't perfect. Just ask our wives. We make many mistakes, and smart wives learn to be good forgivers. We husbands, on the other hand, may forgive ourselves more slowly. God is the God of the clean slate. His word to us is "You're forgiven. Go and sin no more." Forgive yourself for your husbandly faults, and be a better man in the future.

God, I know how often I've not been the best husband I could be. Thank you for the forgiveness I have in Christ. Thank you that all my sins are gone...forever. Thank you, too, for a forgiving wife. Because of the forgiveness I have from you, I forgive myself for my sins and faults. In the future I pray you'll help me sharpen my husbandly abilities. May I be a better husband a year from now.

GOD, THE GREAT RESTORER

I will restore to you the years that the swarming locust has eaten, the hopper, the destroyer, and the cutter, my great army, which I sent among you.
JOEL 2:25

Many married men have a past that's taken a toll on their life. That, in turn, may be having an effect on their marriage. But God has a way of restoring men from their past mistakes, large or small. Trust him to do it for you.

Lord, like most men, I have some things in my life that could use restoration. You know what they are. You know how to restore that area of my life. I ask you to undo the damage I've done. Cause that which was destructive to somehow become a building block for good in my life. Help me learn from my past.

COURTING YOUR WIFE

My beloved speaks and says to me:
"Arise, my love, my beautiful one,
and come away,
for behold, the winter is past;
the rain is over and gone."
SONG OF SOLOMON 2:10-11

When a man and woman show mutual interest, they usually start seeing each other regularly. It used to be *dating*. Before that, it was *courting*. The idea was the man would demonstrate his interest in a woman by "wooing" her with flowers, candy, dinner out, a movie, and words that bespoke his interest.

Once married, the tendency is that such wooing lessens, sometimes even comes to a complete stop as the husband and wife settle into a routine. But a wise husband will continue courting his wife throughout their marriage. Courting, as such, helps keep the flame alive.

Father, you brought me and my wife together for a lifetime of courting. We're a bit settled now, and we don't often get out as much as we used to. The fun of courting is mostly a memory now. Lord, remind us how it felt to be discovering our love for each other. Keep that memory alive, fresh, and young, Lord.

The Praying Marriage

*Rejoice in hope, be patient in
tribulation, be constant in prayer.*
Romans 12:12

Husband, take time to pray not just *for* your wife,
but *with* your wife. Praying couples are staying
couples. You will both have similar burdens for people
you know, crucial situations, perhaps relatives in trouble. Make it a prayer-date ahead of time or you won't
do it. Do this at least weekly, if not daily.

Heavenly Father, prayer is such a great invention of
yours. It is a way to communicate our praise, our needs,
our worries—all with the knowledge that you hear and
are pleased to answer. There is surely great power in
the prayers of couples such as my wife and me. Help
us as we learn to pray together effectively. May we
see great answers to our petitions and rejoice in seeing your hand at work. Give us prayer burdens for others that will result in the advancement of your kingdom.
Lord, make us a great prayer team.

A Soft Answer

*A soft answer turns away wrath, but
a harsh word stirs up anger.*
PROVERBS 15:1

Arguments start when someone speaks in anger. A soft reply usually ends the spat. Become a husband who will not stir up anger with harsh words. Remember, it takes two to tangle.

Lord, help me become a man with the soft answer, turning away the anger stirred up by harsh words. Keep my emotions cool and my mind set on peaceful resolutions to disagreements. When I speak in anger to my wife, it's as though I'm rejecting a gift you've given me. If I respect and honor her as the treasure she is, I'm honoring you.

INTIMACY

The husband should give to his
wife her conjugal rights,
and likewise the wife to her husband.

1 CORINTHIANS 7:3

When our culture exalts sexual intimacy, it's done in a way far removed from God's design. The greatest sexual experience a couple can have is in becoming a giver of pleasure to their spouse, not thinking of their own pleasure. It's as we please our partner that we ourselves experience the full joy of sexual expression. During intimacy with your wife, focus on her responses, not your own. Be a giver, not a taker.

Sex is the ultimate physical expression of our love. That's why God puts a necessary boundary around it. The more a person violates the divine boundaries of sex, the less their ultimate pleasure.

God, your invention of the sexual union between a husband and wife is amazing. When I'm enjoying intimacy with my beloved, help me remember to set my own pleasure aside and focus on pleasing her. Lord, safeguard our sexual union as we live in this sexually saturated culture. Keep us enjoying sex as you created it—with proper boundaries and a sense of how very sacred our "one flesh" intimacy can be.

BOLD FAITH

*In Christ Jesus our Lord, in whom
we have boldness and access with
confidence through our faith in him.*
EPHESIANS 3:12

We Christian men can be too timid sometimes. God has given us boldness and confidence through our faith in him. If we're not being bold, then what's holding us back? Sin? Doubt? Worry? Reject them all—and any other distraction from bold faith. Believe God for great things in your life.

God, thank you that because I have saving faith in you, I also have boldness for life. I can step out prayerfully, unafraid, and be the man you've called me to be. In my boldness, I pray I can be a good leader for our family. Not stubborn or prideful, but confident in *you*, Lord. Fill me now with boldness in those weak areas of my life where I've become too reticent. Bring fruit into my life because of my confidence in you.

The Diligent Husband

The soul of the sluggard craves and gets nothing,
while the soul of the diligent is richly supplied.
PROVERBS 13:4

Husbands must be doers, not just thinkers or planners. We must put feet to our ideas and dreams to make them happen. Many a man has passed through life as merely a dreamer—imagining for himself a life that will never be, unless he follows through on his dreams with diligence.

Father God, you have work for me to do. I pray that I'll be found diligent in accomplishing all you have for me as a man, and as a husband and father. Your Word promises a rich supply for being diligent. I pray as a family man that my diligence as a husband and father will be rewarded by a richly supplied family—a happy and satisfied wife and wise children who have dreams of their own which they, too, will pursue with diligence.

THE CHRISTIAN MIND
OF A HUSBAND

I will meditate on your precepts and
fix my eyes on your ways.
PSALM 119:15

The mind of a Christian works differently than that of an unbeliever. Our worldview coincides with the Bible, not with what the evening news tells us. The Bible is our guidebook for life. Our ways of being a husband and father are sometimes at variance with the culture. The way we do business is not always the standard operating procedure with the rest of the world. But if we're wise, we'll realize that our difference is also our advantage. Think Christianly!

God, daily I'm bombarded with the ways of the world. Help me keep my perspective as a Christian man whose eyes are fixed on your ways, not man's. Speak to me through your Word as I meditate on your precepts. Guide me as I lead my family in accordance with your family plan, not the philosophy of the latest anti-dad sitcom. As I submit my thoughts to you, Lord, purify my mind and my heart. Bring about the results in my life of a man whose ways are pleasing to you.

Enduring Loss

When the righteous cry for help, the LORD hears
and delivers them out of all their troubles. The
LORD is near to the brokenhearted and saves the
crushed in spirit. Many are the afflictions of the
righteous, but the LORD delivers him out of them all.
He keeps all his bones; not one of them is broken.
PSALM 34:17-20

When we go through losses in life, God is there. He is near and he saves us when we are crushed in spirit. Yes, our afflictions may be many, but our God will deliver us out of all of them. He is faithful to His own!

Lord, you are my God not only when times are good, but also when I suffer loss. With you as my deliverer, I will prevail in the end. I pray for you to be near me and my wife as we go through loss. When we are brokenhearted, bind up our wounds. Be near, Lord—very near—when we cry for help.

A Christian's Freedom

*For freedom Christ has set us
free; stand firm therefore,
and do not submit again to a yoke of slavery.*
GALATIANS 5:1

The Galatians were being tempted to go back to the law to please God, but Paul reminded them that they were now free through grace and should act as people who are free. No, this was not freedom *to* sin; it was freedom *from* the power of sin. Once set free, it's foolish to return to our chains—whether those chains are religious legalism, addiction, or false philosophies preached by the world's sages.

God, you have set me free in Christ. I am a free man and a free husband. Free to fully obey you. Free to be the man you've called me to be—and that's something legalism could never achieve. Lord, I pray that each member of our family would be able to embrace the freedom you have for us in Christ. I pray my wife will flourish as a woman in Christ. May your Spirit lead her into her own personal greatness—just as you want to do for all of us.

WORSHIP

*Oh come, let us worship and bow down; let
us kneel before the LORD, our Maker!*
PSALM 95:6

A good worshiper of God will make for a good husband (and father, too, if there are children). Why?
Because a man who worships God realizes two things:
his own smallness in the universe, and the greatness of
the God he serves. Those two truths are liberating.

God, I am but a man. One of your creations. I have
nothing that you did not give me. I have no talents or
abilities that did not originate in you. I praise you for
what you've given me as a man. I praise you for who
you are as my God. There is none like you: majestic,
holy, powerful, eternal, life-giving...all this and so much
more. Today I worship you. Tomorrow I will worship you.
In eternity I will worship you....and thus I am fulfilled.

BUILT FOR BATTLE

You equipped me with strength for the battle;
you made those who rise against me sink under me.
PSALM 18:39

It's natural for most men to want to do battle—to be a warrior for a great cause. And we men do have battles to wage in this life that call forth the warrior spirit within us. Thank God, he equips us for every battle we face. And it is in him alone that we have victory.

Lord, sometimes my life is like a war zone. Even during peaceful times, there's always something that threatens the peace. Thank you that you've called me into battle as a spiritual warrior. You have equipped me for the difficulties I face. You cause those who fight against me to sink beneath me. I do battle, but you bring the victory. Thank you, God, that you declare victory on my behalf even before the battle begins. Because of you, I can enjoy the victor's prize.

DEALING WITH GUILT

Come now, let us reason together, says the
LORD: though your sins are like scarlet, they
shall be as white as snow; though they are red
like crimson, they shall become like wool.
ISAIAH 1:18

A man's sins can consume him unless he is delivered from the power and the penalty for them. Thank God we have a remedy for our sin and the accompanying guilt: the blood of Christ, our Savior. Make use of this—God's only solution to sin. In him, you can find freedom from sin.

Lord, I have sinned often, as you know. As a husband, I know some of my sins have hurt my wife. I rejoice that I can be free from the guilt of my sins through the blood of Christ. I'm also grateful that in some way I don't understand, you can turn my past sins into stepping-stones instead of boulders that cause me to stumble.

LOVING THE CHURCH

*Let us consider how to stir up one another to love
and good works, not neglecting to meet together, as
is the habit of some, but encouraging one another,
and all the more as you see the Day drawing near.*
HEBREWS 10:24-25

The church is the gathering of God's people—his "called out" ones. Many Christians are too quick to find fault with the bride of Christ when they should be binding up her wounds and strengthening her. Don't just attend your church. Be part of its lifeblood.

Lord, I know you love your church, the bride of Christ. I am a part of your church, and I pray for her and support her however I can. When I consider the church as Christ's bride, I think of my own bride and my love for her. If I were to see my bride hurting, I would rush to her side. Lord, empower me to do the same for your bride. Help me do my part to bring healing to your church.

The Husband as Spiritual Guardian of the Home

Put on the whole armor of God, that you may be able to stand against the schemes of the devil.
Ephesians 6:11

A husband is the spiritual guardian of his home. His prayers protect the family from spiritual assault and any other tactic of the enemy to destroy the family. Don't turn this responsibility over to your wife by your passivity. Take seriously the responsibility that God has given you as the head of your household.

Lord, thank you for empowering me to stand guard for my family. I do not take this responsibility lightly, knowing the designs of the enemy to bring discord and injury to my wife and children. I put on the armor you have given me and, in so doing, I stand strong against the schemes of the devil. I pray against his influence and for your protection over our family. I ask this in the name of Christ, who has forever secured victory over Satan.

WISE COMPANIONS

*Whoever walks with the wise becomes wise, but
the companion of fools will suffer harm.*
PROVERBS 13:20

We all know some foolish husbands—men who make wrong decisions about their life, who hurt their wife and children, who don't act like grown men but more like immature teens. The danger is that when they become our companions, they may affect us more than we affect them. That is why we should seek the companionship of men who are wise—so that they might affect us for good, and we ourselves will grow in wisdom.

Father, thank you for wise brothers in the faith—loyal companions who demonstrate by their actions that they are mature men and loyal husbands. I pray for deeper relationships with them so that they may impart their wisdom to me. I pray especially for young, vulnerable husbands who, whether they realize it or not, need a role model to show them how to husband well. Lord, this calling to be a life-mate to my wife is a glorious and fulfilling calling. Thank you that you have so called me. May I prove faithful to you and my wife in every way.

TRADITIONS

So then, brothers, stand firm and hold to the
traditions that you were taught by us, either
by our spoken word or by our letter.
2 THESSALONIANS 2:15

Do you and your wife have some traditions special to just the two of you? Or perhaps a song that is "your song"? A shared life should lead to a lifetime of shared memories and traditions. It need not be something big or extravagant. Often simple traditions are best. A favorite getaway spot where memories are made. A restaurant. Walks together at dusk. Whenever you can, do the things together that will make for memories and traditions for your family.

God, as I search my memory, I can recall a few things that might make for a good tradition for my wife and me. I think of places we went together, good times we had, songs we enjoyed, vacation spots that seemed made just for us. Help me, Lord, to repeat some of those events or to discover ways to establish meaningful traditions that will make fond memories for us. And may you be the invisible third party to our every tradition.

One Shot

[Make] the best use of the time,
because the days are evil.

EPHESIANS 5:16

We all have one shot at life. There are no do-overs after we pass from this planet. We need to get it right now, while we have breath. We need to be the right husband for our wife today. As has been wisely said, "We all go around only once. But if we do it right, once is enough."

Dear Lord, today I'm very aware of my mortality. I have only so much time on this planet to live a good life—to sow seeds that will sprout a bountiful crop. I pray that as I live this life you've gifted me with, I'll redeem the time, realizing just how short my days are. Father, as I live out my role as a husband, help me to live in such a way that on my last day I'll be able to look back and know I did a good job in serving and loving my wife.

GOD IS WRITING THE STORY OF YOUR MARRIAGE

*You formed my inward parts; you knitted
me together in my mother's womb.
I praise you, for I am fearfully
and wonderfully made.*

PSALM 139:13-14

God is a wonderful author. His books of our lives are full of drama, comedy, highs, lows, and frequently the unexpected plot twist. How is the story of your marriage coming along? Can you trust God for the next chapter? Or the final page? God writes great books when he is the Lord of our story.

Father, thank you for writing the story that is my life. My entire history has been under your control. Even the many mistakes I've made can be turned to good as I surrender them to you. Nothing from my past has gone without your notice. Nothing in my present will be wasted as you tell my story. Even the future and whatever it holds is in your capable hands. God, as you write the chapters about my life as a husband, I pray for a great story with a happy ending. Praise you, Lord.

Dads, Lift Up Your Children in Prayer

These daily prayers and words of encouragement will renew your soul as you intercede in key areas of your child's life, such as

- learning to forgive
- growing spiritually
- developing friendships

Take a minute out of your day to thank God for your children and let him equip you for the challenges of fatherhood with these brief-but-powerful prayers that will easily fit into your busy schedule.

About Nick Harrison

Nick Harrison is the author of more than a dozen books, including *One-Minute Prayers® for Dads* and *Promises to Keep: Daily Devotions for Men Seeking Integrity*. Nick and his wife, Beverly, live in Oregon and are the parents of three adult daughters and grandparents of four grandchildren. Nick's website and blog can be found at nickharrisonbooks.com